ADVANCE PRAISE

"We all desire a journey of self-awareness that reveals a deeper purpose that truly matters. Mark chronicles this journey for us, offering timeless principles that help each of us to lead in very uncertain times."

—Nick Craig, President, Authentic Leadership Institute; best-selling author of *Finding Your True North* and *The Discover Your True North Fieldbook*

"Mark Nation is fascinated with the idea that each of us is made for amazing—that is, by being placed in this world, we are obligated to find, develop, and contribute the best we have of ourselves. He has woven this concept into an absorbing tale that will have readers delving into their own possibilities, as they follow the struggles of a gifted musician to discover the music his beloved grampa always knew was in him."

—James Ballard, best-selling author of *Whale Done!* and *What's the Rush?*

"Mark Nation's extended parable underscores the importance of finding one's authentic self—and the effort that's often required to find it. Unlike many parables that cause the reader to discover key points, Nation offers a gentler form of guidance through the questions he poses outside the narrative. A very helpful addition to the body of self-discovery literature."

—Warren Radtke, founding principal, Right Management Consultants; Episcopal minister

"*Made for Amazing* is a great resource for entrepreneurs, start-ups, and anyone who desires to build a strong and enduring brand. A vital framework for personal and corporate growth."

—**Charlie Brock, CEO, Launch Tennessee**

"The story of a young man and his grandfather is very powerful, as my grandfather was so 'instrumental' in my own life. Music is a brilliant metaphor for encouraging us to 'find our song' and build a purposeful life. Through Josh's grandpa, Mark Nation suggests that *we* are the instruments; what a great way to inspire others to identify and develop the music they were meant to play."

—**Kevin Head, Senior Pastor, First Baptist Roswell; cofounder, New Perspectives for Life**

"Finding your authentic purpose is critical to maintaining vibrant careers and healthy lives. Through Josh Lynk's 'musical' journey, Nation offers at least twenty rock-solid building blocks on how to make an authentic life—indeed, an amazing life—truly possible."

—**Jack Studer, Chairman, Erlanger Health System (rated 9th-best US public hospital)**

"*Made for Amazing* is a rich mixture of self-leadership, philosophy, and spirituality, all wrapped inside an entertaining business parable. The messages contained in this book couldn't be more timely for both Eastern and Western audiences. I am anxious to share Mark's messages with my clients, colleagues, and friends."

—**Charles Ferguson, President, Asia Pacific, ADP (Singapore)**

"The most important questions are the ones you ask yourself, as they hold the keys to discerning the life you were made for. This book is your invitation to an amazing life."

—Bernie Swain, author of *What Made Me Who I Am* and cofounder of Washington Speakers Bureau

"If you're a doer who has forgotten to dream; if you focus on others to the exclusion of living the amazing life you were made for; or if you just want to be more, then read this book now."

—Rob Bernshteyn, CEO, Coupa Software; author of *Value as a Service*

"Mark Nation is a rare, renaissance leader—professional musician, Harvard MBA, global executive, leadership coach, Ironman triathlete. He has applied his unique talents and experiences to craft a compelling and big-hearted story that resonates with a timeless, yet very timely, truth: The pursuit of fame and fortune can steal your soul and leave you empty, when you do not replenish your life with faith, family, friends, and song. Song is, of course, a metaphor for the true voice that is calling you, and—trust me on this—Mark *will help you* to find the song you are meant to sing. *Made for Amazing* is told with grace, compassion, pathos, and heart; the story will move you to tears, then lift you up with the encouragement needed to renew your search for deeper meaning and purpose. It's a joy to read and, most importantly, filled with a message we really need to take seriously—now more than ever."

—Jim Kouzes, Dean's Executive Fellow of Leadership, Leavey School of Business, Santa Clara University; coauthor of the best-selling book, *The Leadership Challenge*

"If you're ready to bring something amazing to life instead of letting life 'happen' to you, *read this book*. *Made for Amazing* contains powerful, inspiring, even eternal, principles that will lift your heart and mind toward God's incredible plans for you. Prepare to be blessed!"

—Bonnie Wurzbacher, former Chief Resource Development Officer, World Vision International; former Senior VP, Global Customer & Channel Leadership, The Coca-Cola Company

"As a musician and business leader, I have always described the essence of leadership with the visual of a choral director aligning the voices of a talented choir. And now, in this beautiful story, our souls are once again reminded that each individual is uniquely designed by God, with an amazing song to sing. Imagine the possibilities if everyone simply understood that notion. Read *Made for Amazing*, refresh your spirit, and let your soul burst forth with a bold, new tune."

—Cheryl A. Bachelder, former CEO, Popeyes Louisiana Kitchen, Inc.; author of *Dare to Serve*

"I sincerely believe our greatest challenge in life is to live up to our God-given potential and be our best self, and Mark has created a unique roadmap for each of us to do so. His authenticity, passion, and perspective shine through, acting as a guiding light for all of us to find our signal amidst the noise."

—Anoop Prakash, Managing Director, Harley-Davidson Canada and India

"Every once in a while, an author and book come along and shake up the landscape of the human spirit. For me, Mark Nation is that author, and *Made for Amazing* is that book."

—Jose Antonio La Rosa, CEO, Supera (Peru)

"In our increasingly complex and volatile world, it's easy to lose sight of what's most important. We should always strive to 'keep the main thing the main thing,' as the soul is at least as important as the goal. There is no more interesting way to discover this truth than through Mark's amazing book and world-class leadership coaching. If you have any desire to instill values, integrity, and that 'something more' in your career and business, then *Made for Amazing* should be added to your top shelf. A leadership classic."

—Peter Lowe, founder, Get Motivated! seminars

"Inspirational leadership is within all of us, and in *Made for Amazing*, Mark Nation urges us to find and sharpen it. By using our unique, God-given talents, and learning from both mentors and past mistakes, we can tame the negative influences that surround us continually—including our own self-doubts. Mark illuminates the path to inspirational leadership, offers the keys to unlock an amazing career, and frees us to impact the lives of others in profound and enduring ways. I loved this book."

—Kevin Rabbitt, CEO, NEP, broadcast services producer for the Olympics, NFL, NBA, MLB, and major entertainment and award shows worldwide

"If you liked *The Purpose-Driven Life* and *Finding Your True North*, then you *must* get your hands on this book. In *Made for Amazing*, I felt like Mark Nation was sitting between Rick Warren and Bill George, bringing the very best of their concepts all together. An incredibly fresh and compelling read."

—Cordell Carter, II, Eisenhower Fellow; White House Champion of Change; Executive Director, The Aspen Institute; former Chief of Staff, Bill and Melinda Gates Foundation

"Mark has some of the most powerful assessments and tools I have ever used. In addition, he has an uncanny ability to synthesize leadership stories and call out those unique patterns that bring strength and deeper purpose to life. He has drawn from decades of experience to create a book that is as poignant and uplifting as it is entertaining. I find myself using Mark's innovative concepts and ideas constantly with my teams, and soon you will be doing the same."

—**Shauna McIntyre, People Operations and Program Management Executive, Google; former automotive executive, Egon Zehnder International and Ford Motor Company**

"Mark Nation might actually qualify as the most interesting man in the world. His eclectic career has granted him an almost unparalleled perspective on business, faith, and the world. This book channels a bit of it all. It's a work of art."

—**Johnnie Moore, founder, The KAIROS Company; former Chief of Staff and Vice President, United Artists Media Group**

"I was initially skeptical of a book that promised so much in its title. Who doesn't want to be amazing? However, most of us are trained to believe 'amazing' is a benefit offered exclusively to a select few. In this inspiring story, Mark Nation opens the possibility of 'amazing' to each of us; most important, he shows us the way to discover an amazing career and fulfilling life. The last thing we want is to wake up one day, saying, 'I wish I had done this differently.' Thanks to Mark for taking the time to write this book, inspiring us all to take positive action before it is too late."

—**Paula Pontes, Global General Manager, GLAMGLOW®; former GM, Estee Lauder Companies (Brazil)**

"Mark Nation has captured that rarest of all images—a snapshot of our heart's deepest desires. Disappointment happens to all of us . . . and it takes a special guide who can free us to soar on the musical notes of our God-given symphony. Dare to sing your *own* song. Dare to lead an *amazing* life. Trust Mark and this book to be your guides."

—Paul Louis Cole, President, Christian Men's Network Worldwide; founding pastor, C3 Church

"I love the title, *Made for Amazing*, because it accurately states the possibility within each of us to live an amazing life. What holds so many of us back? This is a question of incredible importance. What if we begin a journey to simply trust that God will help us overcome our fear, give up selfish ambition, let go of instant gratification, and do what we know is right? *Made for Amazing* will encourage you to step out and be, yes *be*, who you were made to be, rather than defining yourself by what you do."

—Frank Brock, former President, Covenant College; former co-owner, Brock Candy

"My grandmother used an antique recipe for making wonderful hasenpfeffer (rabbit stew). Step 1 read, 'First, get a rabbit!' *Made for Amazing* is like a recipe for personal greatness but with a vital step added. Mark Nation's special recipe for authentic leadership transformation will help you obtain your own version of the first step in my grandmother's recipe. If you only read two books this year, I recommend reading this book twice!"

—Chip R. Bell, best-selling author of *Kaleidoscope* and *Sprinkles*

MADE

FOR

AMAZING

MADE
FOR
AMAZING

AN INSTRUMENTAL JOURNEY *of*
AUTHENTIC LEADERSHIP TRANSFORMATION

MARK NATION

GREENLEAF
BOOK GROUP PRESS

Published by Greenleaf Book Group Press
Austin, Texas
www.gbgpress.com

Copyright ©2017 Mark Nation

Distributed by Greenleaf Book Group

For ordering information or special discounts for bulk purchases, please contact Greenleaf Book Group at PO Box 91869, Austin, TX 78709, 512.891.6100.

Design and composition by Greenleaf Book Group
Cover design by Greenleaf Book Group
Cover images: © Martin Capek, Artography, and Travis Allen. Used under license from Shutterstock.com

Scripture taken from the *New American Standard Bible*®. Copyright © 1960, 1962, 1963, 1968, 1973, 1975, 1977, 1995 by The Lockman Foundation. Used by permission.

Scripture taken from the *New King James Version*®. Copyright © 1982 by Thomas Nelson. Used by permission. All rights reserved.

Cataloging-in-Publication data is available.

Print ISBN: 978-1-62634-481-5

eBook ISBN: 978-1-62634-482-2

Part of the Tree Neutral® program, which offsets the number of trees consumed in the production and printing of this book by taking proactive steps, such as planting trees in direct proportion to the number of trees used: www.treeneutral.com

TreeNeutral˚

Printed in the United States of America on acid-free paper

17 18 19 20 21 22   10 9 8 7 6 5 4 3 2 1

First Edition

To all the incredible people I have had the great pleasure of meeting;
To all the incredible people I have yet to meet (but someday will); and
To all the incredible people I may never have the chance to meet:

This book is dedicated to You.

If we could talk—if I could somehow just get to you—then I would
most certainly tell you:

You Are Amazing.

And you would believe me. I pray that you believe me.

CONTENTS

WHAT ARE YOU MADE FOR?

Your life *matters*. You are designed for a *purpose*.

You are a *Masterpiece*—created for great works that have already been planned for you. In the entire history of the world, no one has ever been made like you, nor will anyone ever be like you again. Your unique and special gifts are straight from the heavens above, and the world needs you desperately. Indeed, you are a vital part of a Grand Plan.

You are not made for a mediocre life; you are built to *thrive*. You are made to be bold and do mighty things that bring about positive, enduring change in our world.

You are Made for *AMAZING*.

INTRODUCTION

The fact that you hold this book in your hands means you are very special to me. I have debated at length as to what I might say to you, were we to meet through the pages of a book. After all, it's incredibly difficult to distill decades of life into a few pages and then call it any sort of instructive manual or representative sample. Nevertheless, I tried to imagine getting one chance to meet with you, just one opportunity to speak to your mind, heart, and soul. *Made for Amazing* is what came to me, and I sincerely hope it will resonate with you on some level.

Those who know me will tell you I love to ask questions. They help me to learn so much about myself as well as businesses and teams, my surroundings, my work and family, other people, and life. Therefore, I've added some introductory material to help you understand a little more about the book—and about me—before you embark on your journey.

Not surprisingly, it's easiest if I think about this material in response to the questions you may ask of me.

WHY A STORY ABOUT A MUSICIAN?

Made for Amazing traces the journey of Joshua Lynk, a talented young musician who struggles to discover his voice and the music he was meant to play to the world. Josh's journey inspires readers to find their own "song"; that is, their authentic leadership and life purpose. The story also encourages us to overcome personal limitations, to combat mental resistance, and to believe we can benefit others in a way that truly "brings amazing to life." It's not a book about music, however; it's a book about *finding your song at work and in life.*

I wrote *Made for Amazing* as a parable, so I could employ subtle, more nuanced methods to offer readers guidance and encouragement. This approach allowed me to craft a story that can entertain many different types of readers, utilizing timeless principles and emotions which music so universally brings to life. Through this "lyrical" journey, the narrative poses thought-provoking questions and offers a variety of teachable moments that unfold naturally over time.

Music is one of life's rare "larger than life" themes; it is as old as history itself, residing in virtually every living element. Like the wind or love, you cannot see music, but you know it when you feel it. Music can soothe the soul, reach broadly with its messages, spark creative dialogue, build character, and enhance self-esteem. We all recognize the visceral emotion a song evokes as it touches our hearts and moves our spirits. *Made for Amazing* employs music as a metaphor to help reunite us—with our world, our communities, our companies, our families . . . and with ourselves.

WHY DID YOU WRITE THIS BOOK?

I am convinced that life and work are meant to be experienced as "superlatives," and that everyone possesses unique gifts that make the extraordinary possible. Unfortunately, so many people in today's world are confused, hurt, broken, or simply have no song in their hearts. Perhaps they have not listened closely enough for the "music in their lives."

I have witnessed this tragic condition in many diverse places around the world, from the mud-structured streets outside Phnom Penh to the glistening avenues of Beverly Hills. In more cases than I ever imagined, people and businesses must be built, or rebuilt, from the ground up, from the inside out. Indeed, a heart-and-soul-centered effort may be what is required to make an amazing life and enduring legacy truly possible.

Made for Amazing was created to help people identify and sharpen their unique talents, both in the workplace and across the broader community. In doing so, they release infinite energies to connect with teammates, customers, family, friends, and others in a very powerful and enduring way. The book is an earnest attempt to help people believe in themselves and their unique abilities, and encourage them to spend their lives honing their incredible talents in a way that contributes positively to the world.

WHERE ARE ALL THE "ANSWERS"?

We know instinctively that key learnings can appear through the questions we ask as often as the answers we receive. In *Made for Amazing*, I simply aimed to "start the conversation," and to guide people to meaningful questions and worthwhile discussion topics. In the book, as in life, there are *few clear, easy* answers. Consequently, Josh's story is not meant to promise quick fixes nor dispense magic, one-size-fits-all solutions. Instead, we each must find our own unique pathway, self-managing the effort to discover and create meaning as it emerges within and around us. Thankfully, helpers always seem to appear to aid and assist us along the way. As I often tell people, the *Joy is in the Journey*.

In thinking about topics to inform and guide deeper learning, I reread the story—and captured more than three hundred questions! I chose to place a select few sample questions at the end of the book, so as not to disrupt the story's flow. This approach provides readers the choice to review and reflect on questions after reading each chapter, or to keep turning the page and allow the questions to emerge at another time. Never underestimate the power of a question to amplify very basic concepts!

HOW SHOULD I READ THE STORY?

I encourage you to approach Josh's story with an open mind, knowing there is almost always a "story within the story." In the opening scenes, you will get a glimpse into Josh's life and his current state of affairs. Then, we will trace Josh's journey from his childhood days to the present time where we first met him. Later in the book, we return to Josh in his present state and then walk alongside him through the rest of his epic journey.

As the storyline unfolds, try to see the story in your mind's eye; take the opportunity to escape your own movie and enter Josh's for just a few moments. Sense the sights and sounds. Feel the tension. Notice word choices, and the "spaces between the notes." Review the chapter questions for more insight, and reread sections of the book when needed to inform deeper self-reflection. Ruminate on the key storyline concepts, then personalize and adapt Josh's story to your own.

Made for Amazing can simply be a source for reading entertainment, but it's really meant to be an *action guide*. It's about Josh's story, but also *your story*. So, please take notes to capture your thoughts and ideas, or consider purchasing the supplementary workbook and materials to gain further insights into your own journey and your own authentic leadership purpose. Like anything in life, the more of yourself you invest into this book, the more you will get out of it. This I can assure you.

WHAT ELSE SHOULD I KNOW?

I intended *Made for Amazing* to be a short and simple story, with a tightly packed mix of both grandiose and granular moments that together inform an enduring quest for inquiry and learning—a sort of "miniature traveler's companion." In this way, I suppose the book represents a humble gift, a spirited adventure, a heartfelt exhortation, and a simple prayer—that those who read the book will in some way be touched. It is my greatest desire that in quietness and stillness, readers will find their own strength, hear the incredible song from within that's calling out to be played—and choose to become "musicians for life."

I welcome your thoughts, questions, and insights, and would love to hear from you. Please post your feedback about the book, and share how your own transformation is unfolding. Let's find some way to talk.

Meanwhile, please consider at least five other special people who will be placed on your heart as you read this book, and choose to *invest yourself* into them. Write them a letter, email or call them, or perhaps even offer them a copy of this book as a gift. Find a way to help them believe they are *amazing*. Write their names down, and then tell me who you selected, and why they came to mind. Trust me, this activity will become a critical part of your own leadership transformation process. *Never underestimate the power of a few simple, heartfelt words, well placed.*

I hope one day we will have the chance to meet, or to meet again. I would love the opportunity to thank you for your time and investment, both in me and in yourself. Believe me when I say *you are worth it*. I look forward to the day we can shake hands or share a friendly hug, when I can admire you in person and see the *amazing* one in you.

Our chief want is someone who will inspire
us to be what we know we could be.

—*Ralph Waldo Emerson*

CHAPTER 1

GRAMPA

"HEAD FOR AP JACK!"

Joshua Lynk sat bolt upright in bed, heart beating wildly, eyes staring into the darkness. Was it a dream, or had he been *there*? There again, in a boat on a lake in the worst freak storm of the summer! It seemed he could still feel the spray stinging his face. Near the shore in his dream, trees were falling, boats crashing into docks, lightning drenching the place in light, and the lake seeming to lift to meet the downpour. A panic-stricken boy of nine in those revisited dream moments, all he had wished for was the warmth and safety of his grandfather's cabin. But the old man's shout from the kayak churning the waves beside him gave him his direction, and he obediently dug for the mountain.

As Joshua's breath calmed, his mind strove to hang onto the fading images that had swept him back to a moment twenty-five years before: his kayak tossed about like a chip in the waves, the mountain bulking dimly through the downpour. Mostly, he wanted to keep the feeling of that presence in the other boat, the one with the reassuring voice, the one who always knew what to do. He tried to recreate the face he'd seen faintly for the first time in years, but he couldn't bring it into focus. The dream was fading, but it was with him still to the extent that his breath caught in a sudden sob.

Joshua Lynk had once been "somebody," but these days he considered himself another washed-up musician, down on his luck and forgotten. Having been a top performer for ten years, and a star for over three, he was now living day-to-day in a state of numbness, bewildered by the way things had turned out. These days, his existence as a mere guitar teacher on the outskirts of Seattle seemed humdrum, marginal. For the millionth time, he asked himself, *How has such a magnificent run ended in such a wreck?*

He rose dully, blighted by sleep and depression, still troubled by the lake dream. He went to the tiny kitchen and poured a cup of coffee. He took a sip and grimaced. *Like my life*, he thought. *Cold and stale.* On impulse, he sat down at the table and pulled his laptop to him and Googled "Ap Jack Mountain."

There it was, that once well-loved peak near Tenby, Washington, with the lake at its foot. Josh read the caption: "Nicknamed Ap Jack by some of the older Welsh summer residents, the mountain's real name is Mount Tevilo." This he had not known growing up, for between him and his grandfather the Pacific Northwestern mountain was, ever and always, Ap Jack. Summer after summer, the old man had told him stories about the mountain, shaped like a minor Matterhorn, that rose across the lake and charmed the boy with its romance. Grampa had taught him to watch the mountain and notice how it was different each time they looked, with the sun on the rocks at the top, the deep green forest on its rolling flanks, and cloud shadows playing across it.

Joshua closed the laptop, took a scrap of paper, and scribbled idly on it the only remainder he had of the dream: *Head for Ap Jack!* He smiled sarcastically, thinking, *God knows there's little enough to color my days now. Same boring routine. Kids who don't want to learn, who'll never learn to play or be any good. The few bucks I make are hardly a reason to perpetuate this stupid existence, but what else would I, could I, be doing at this point in my good-for-nothing life?*

Grampa. The once-beloved elder had hardly crossed Joshua's mind in the years since the old man's passing. *Out of sight, out of mind*, he thought, and thinking it he felt ashamed at the long stretch since he had revisited thoughts of his grandfather.

Now that the memories rushed back to him, it was the crwth, of course, that stood out. Carved and shaped lovingly by his Welsh grampa, the precious stringed instrument from his homeland, together with the tunes the old man could bring from it, fascinated Josh as a youngster. Bowing it skillfully into the shape of what looked to Josh like his own toy bow and arrow, Brynmor Lynk would coax a seemingly endless variety of melodies from its gleaming fingerboard. The old man's playing had been Josh's introduction to music.

Sometimes, Bryn would be joined on the crwth by his old friend Gerwyn Jones, a gifted flutist who lived across the lake. A traditional lullaby called "Suo Gan" was Josh's favorite. Whenever he listened to Gerwyn's plaintive flute trilling the notes of that song, Josh seemed to rise out of himself, his eyes brimming over helplessly. Other times, his toes would tap as Gerwyn and Grampa beat out "Caniad Y Gwyn Bibydd" (The Song of the White Piper), a brisk dance tune hundreds of years old. Young Josh didn't understand how the music could do these things to him, but his grampa did. Often, Josh would see those gray eyes beneath the shock of white hair looking searchingly at him, as if to discern something he saw in Josh's response to the music.

Josh's mother, May, could play anything by ear on the piano. People would often gather in their home to sing old Welsh hymns in their minor keys, and the soaring strains would lift the boy's heart. When he was small, his grampa used to lift Josh up onto the piano and have the people sing "Joshua Fought the Battle of Jericho." Most of the folks were not Welsh-speaking, but a few were. So, Josh learned most of the minor songs in English. His favorites were the gospel-sounding tunes like "Go Down Moses" and "Go Tell It on the Mountain." His favorite hymn of all was "In the Garden"; he was drawn to the story it told and the devotion it expressed. At the end of a particularly spiritual song, the folks would sometimes smile, nod, and repeat soulfully, *Canu gyda ysbryd*, meaning "Sung with the spirit."

Josh could go to his mother with any new song he'd heard at school or out at play, sit her down at the piano, and hum the song. May could then play it, chords and all, in that same key, never having heard it before. Josh Lynk grew up in an atmosphere of music being made.

. . .

As he sat at the table now, another memory, long treasured but long forgotten, came to him from a Christmas long ago . . .

"One at a time, children," his mother chided. "We wait while each person takes a turn to open a gift." Josh and his older sister, Alwyn, had been arguing over whose turn it was.

"Oh, Ma, there aren't that many gifts, anyway!" Josh said impatiently. His grampa's squint directed its gaze to his mother's hurt look and Josh regretted his thoughtless remark. This little family had to be, as May Lynk would say, careful with its pennies. Her earnings as a salesperson at a downtown dry-goods store, supplemented by Bryn's meager pension from his years as a mail carrier, barely met expenses. In his later years, Bryn had taken on additional work as a luthier—a builder and restorer of wooden instruments—to bridge the income gap.

May finished opening a gift from her father-in-law, a hand-carved loon Bryn had made. There was a pause; then, taking an oblong box from behind the tiny tree, the old man said, "For you, Josh."

"Wow!" Josh exulted, attacking the box. He lifted out a

shining blond ukulele and, mouth open, looked wonderingly at his grampa. "You carved it, didn't you, Grampa?"

"It's because of what's within ya, lad," Bryn said, his gray eyes twinkling.

"What's within ya" was a phrase Josh had heard before from the old man. It puzzled him. This morning he decided to ask, "What do you mean, 'within me,' Grampa?"

The old man said, "Hush now. I think it's my own turn!"

. . .

Josh had known his father, William, only until he was seven, when the man had left suddenly, for good. Before his departure, he'd seemed to have little or no time for the family, spending most of his time at his job as a bartender. Josh's memories of his father focused on his sharpness and impatience. Having seen his grampa bowing his head silently before meals, Josh had once ventured to ask, "Daddy, is there a God?"

"No!" came the definitive answer.

Tears rose. "But I want to meet Him!"

"If you ever met God, you would go crazy," William said and walked away. Perhaps it was from his father that Josh had inherited his temper and sharp tongue. He shook his head now. This review of past vanities the frightening dream had occasioned was not to his liking. He stood up, turned out the kitchen light, and crept back to his lonely bed.

The doorbell rang, jolting Joshua awake. Groggily realizing it was late morning, he quickly dressed and went to the door to greet Sam, his twelve-year-old guitar student. He was never glad to see this boy, one of the "sent" ones with little interest of his own, whose parents wanted him to learn an instrument. Sam heaved a sigh as he came in the door, tossing his baseball glove disgustedly onto a chair. "This sucks!" he groused. "We were ahead, and I had to leave." *The joys of a music teacher*, thought Joshua as he led the way to the practice room. Then came a second thought: *I should talk. I used to be that way myself with the maestro.* Again, the choking sense of futility clouded his brain. *What am I doing here, anyway?*

. . .

Later that afternoon, Joshua was sitting idly in his car, waiting in a fast-food order lane, when the thought came of how it had all started with the ukulele. "That's it. You're getting it," Bryn Lynk told his grandson, as Josh tried to fit his fingers into the three basic chording positions his grampa had shown him on the ukulele. "This is hard," Josh complained. "My fingers are sore, and I don't even know why I'm working on this dumb ukulele, instead of on a real guitar."

The old man reached over and took the instrument from him. He began to pick out an older Welsh tune called "Amapola," which Josh had heard played on the radio. Bryn's tremolo fingerpicking technique and buttery fretboard movements sustained the notes of the song and made the ukulele come alive. The tiny instrument seemed to instantly have been transformed into a small orchestra.

Something very lyrical and elegant is looking for you.

When the performance ended, Josh was bursting with excitement at what the old man had done. "Wow!" he said. "How did you learn to play like that, Grampa? I thought you only played the crwth."

"Listen here, boy—something very lyrical and elegant is looking for you," Bryn said, now pointing a finger at Josh. "You thought the ukulele can't make the music!" He shook his head. "It's not the ukulele that can't make it; it's you; it's me. We don't make the music because we're not in tune." He saw the boy's confusion. "You—how do I tell you?"

We don't make the music because we're not in tune.

"Tell me what?"

"How it's we who are the instruments."

Josh laughed. "If we're instruments, who is playing us?" he asked.

The old man pointed to the sky.

"You mean God?"

"Who else? We are the instruments, and God is the Master Player. When *we* are in tune, He plays through *us*."

"Grampa, you're funny. You say I'm an instrument, and you tell me I have to get in tune. How do I do that? How do I get in tune?"

But the old man looked away with a shake of his head. No more discussion on that subject. "You thought the ukulele didn't make the music," he said, handing the instrument back to Josh. "This makes the music when you make the music!"

Josh looked with new care and respect at the device his grampa's hands had shaped, from which he had just coaxed such sounds. "I could never learn to play like you, Grampa."

The old man gazed at the boy until he met his eyes again. "Not yet," was all he said.

Joshua Lynk was glad when the lesson was finished and Sam had returned to his ball game. He took up a pile of song sheets from the table and went to his car. Driving to another student's home for his second scheduled lesson of the day, he mused, *This won't be bad. Dotty's a brighter kid, both in intelligence and attitude.*

On the way home after the lesson with Dotty, it was unseasonably hot; Joshua put the windows down. The music sheets on the seat beside him rustled in the wind. As he moved them, the breeze picked up a scrap of paper that had been under the sheets and blew it in front of his face. He caught the tiny scrap just before it went out the window. He looked at the phrase penciled on it.

"I could do it," he said aloud. "I could start out now and be there by dark." Without warning, such a tide of grief rose in his chest that he had to pull the car to the side of the road. He got out, walked into a field, doubled over, and grabbed his stomach, great sobs shaking him uncontrollably. Memories came trooping back of all the summers he had spent up at the lake with his wife, Joy, when the girls were small. Family games and concerts, campfires, kayaking and sailing. Three years of separation now. Beth preparing for high school; Sarah Grace now in elementary school. It was all gone, gone down the toilet.

I'm lost, he thought. A tortured wail rose out of him: *"Grampa!"*

Nothing ever comes to one, that is worth having,
except as a result of hard work.

—*Booker T. Washington*

CHAPTER 2

MONDAYS WITH THE MAESTRO

"TRY IT AGAIN."

The patient, direct tone of his teacher's baritone voice always arrested Josh's attention, compelling him to respond obediently. What was it Grampa had said? "The man is not frightening. He just means business." Peter Colesworthy was a former concert pianist of renown, and his prowess as a classical guitarist was equally notable. Several of his students had risen to fame.

Today, as usual, young Josh just wanted his guitar lesson to be over. Mr. C was too demanding, too painstaking! As far as Josh was concerned, he'd done the figure right that time—the *third* time! He looked at the thin features, the unblinking eyes behind the horn-rimmed glasses, the long aristocratic nose above a dark, carefully trimmed moustache. But his teacher's wardrobe was the most arresting. No one else Josh had ever met wore a white linen suit, which always seemed crisp and freshly laundered. The way his teacher looked demanded respect.

As he moved to play the line again, he heard, "Wait." He paused while Mr. Colesworthy corrected the position of his fingering arm, rounding his wrist until it hurt. "Hold it there, hum."

Josh sighed loudly, knowing it would not faze his teacher, who said, "It's foundational. No muscles in the fingers, hum." Now he felt a small nudge on his left shoulder blade. "Keep the x-y axis with shoulders and spine, Josh."

Why classical *guitar*? Josh's mind complained. *I want to play jazz. I want to play rock!*

"Every true kind of guitar craftsmanship must be built on these basics," hummed Mr. C. "They form the architecture of good performance."

How does he know what I'm thinking? Josh wondered.

Peter Colesworthy watched the boy writhing on the stool in front of him. His commitment to his calling did not allow him to react to the surface behavior of his students—the agony over details; the impatience to "just play" that dulled their ability to bring what they had from within, and which led so many into mediocrity. Peter's gift kept him up at night, for he heard the music that was in people and he could not turn it off. His calling was to release it in a chosen few.

As a master, Peter Colesworthy was on the lookout for a

student who had some inkling of the music that was truly his or hers, the gift he or she had to give. *They do not know they have it*, he thought. *They just feel something. Usually it expresses as a wish to perform. They've seen the limelight and they want it. Fame-seeking can be the blighting of their gift. I must find a way to strengthen the knowing I see in this one. I expect impatience with beginners, but this boy's lack of concentration could likely work against the extraordinary promise I see. I must hold him to a high standard without reining in his will to be good, to be the best.*

Peter knew he must challenge his budding prodigy to follow his dream. It was there, but it was at risk. These were the days that counted. He must be careful, lest the boy throw the lessons over, and the god of ordinariness claims another.

One clue that surfaced early was a natural *rubato*, an expressive and rhythmic freedom the master recognized in a slight speeding up and slowing down of the tempo of a piece at the boy's own discretion. Peter marveled to see this intuitive timing in one so young. *It has been a long time*, he told himself, *since I've had one that promises to move audiences.*

"And *breathe*, Josh! Breathing is the house we sit on."

"But I'm not singing!"

"Whether you sing or not—and you will sing, hum!— you must find a seat in the breath and feel your center there."

"It's too much to think about! Besides, I don't have a seat inside me."

"You do, but it's an empty chair, waiting for someone, hum,

you don't know you are. Don't think. *Feel!* Your brain is merely an outpost. Your music comes from the center of you."

"Where's that?"

"Exactly. Now, once again, hum."

Don't think. *Feel!* Your brain is merely an outpost. Your music comes from the center of you.

Josh was putting his guitar in the case by the front door when the master approached and said, "Do you know your mother wants to sign you up for the next ten lessons?"

Long pause. "Yes."

"I want to know what you think, Josh. Sometimes I think you're fighting me."

"It's not you."

"All right. But you need to know that you're far enough I can see that you are ready."

"Ready for what? I've barely started."

"But you are ahead of the usual story. You are at what I call the cusp. Lots of students quit where you are right now. The choice to go on is a critical one. It means either that you'll continue to give proper care to your technique, or you won't."

"I know, but it's hard."

"It will get harder." The teacher paused. "What do you want, Josh?"

"I want to play steel!"

"Hum. Think about it, Josh. For you, I see . . ." He turned and walked away.

. . .

"Dude! I thought you'd never get outta there! I hate it when that guy keeps you late!" Danny Goldsmith was doing his usual complaining about waiting for Josh to finish his lesson.

"It wasn't too bad today. I learned a lot. And hey, call him Mr. C."

"Mm. How about we call him the Maestro? That's a term of respect, and he looks like he should be conducting an orchestra." Seeing Josh smile, his best friend continued: "Let's go down to Sander's Music and listen to CDs. Jake's on today and he'll let us use the headphones; I can't wait to hear the new Aerosmith!"

"*Aerosmith!* Listen, Danny, your drumming suffers when you listen to all that bashing. You're a steady backbeat drummer. Nobody touches you when you're in the pocket."

"Yeah, you're right. I just like their songs. What are you gonna hear?"

"Me? The usual. Clapton, Steely Dan, Greg Allman, Santana."

"Santana! Dude, you're gonna wear that album out! It's at least ten years old now!"

"Sure. That's why it's good. Nobody plays like Carlos Santana. I think it's timeless. I can play every one of his solos now."

A few days before Josh's birthday, he overheard his grand-father on the telephone, saying, almost in a whisper, "Yes. The check for the next lessons is in the mail." The old man hurriedly hung up and gave Josh their usual parting hug. Throughout the day, Josh thought about it. He resolved to speak to his grandpa about his conflict with the style and rigor of the guitar lessons. After school, he went to his grand-father's shop. The old man was busy lightly sanding the body of a new mahogany guitar.

"Grampa," he said, "I'm confused."

"Mm," the old man murmured dismissively.

"I'm learning classical guitar on a used guitar you are renting for me. But I want to play popular music with a band. How will I ever be able to switch over?"

Grampa went on sanding. Finally, he said, "Seems to me, if you work hard every day practicing what you learn in your lessons, your dream will follow."

"But how?" Josh asked. "How will it follow?"

The old man paused in his work. "By the power of inten-tion, Josh. Intention works like a law. It is behind every-thing you see in the world. God demonstrates it by creating a world that goes on working before our eyes, turning the seasons, growing trees and plants, giving us air and water and food. Likewise, intention is in every so-called man-made object. For instance, look at this guitar I'm making. How do you think it is getting made?"

Josh looked at the gleaming mahogany neck, folded into the ash wood body of a beautiful guitar. "Um, by your intention?"

"Exactly. So, if you connect your intention to play in a

band with your hard work practicing what you're learning from Mr. C, the law will work."

Josh shook his head. "I don't get it, Grampa," he said. "How can one thing lead to the oth—"

"Okay," the old man said, turning away. "Too much talk. I am busy. Scoot now."

. . .

That was a birthday Josh would remember all his life. The beautiful guitar his grandfather had been fashioning so carefully that day in his shop was his! He was choked with awe when his grampa laid the gleaming instrument in his hands.

"Steel!" Josh kept saying. "Steel!"

"Sure. Steel!" Grampa said.

"This'll take a pickup fine," Josh exulted. "And it will sound great through an amplifier with some reverb. Maybe I can even learn slide! I'm going to name it my Old Warrior in honor of you. Oh, Grampa!" Looking into those gray eyes under the bushy eyebrows, Josh saw the love shining in them.

"Its voice will open up nicely over time," Grampa offered. "If you take good care of it, then it'll develop a deeper, richer, and sweeter tone with each passing year." Well pleased with his captive young enthusiast, Grampa continued sharing his thoughts: "Remember what I said about intention?" Josh nodded. "And also what I've told you about us being instruments? It was *your* intention, boy, that worked through my hands to build something that would further your dream. I saw you working hard on your classical practice. That work translated into the work I did to make this guitar. I was allowed to be an instrument for the great music you will one day please so many people with. You see, Josh, when intention is strong and pure, beautiful things are created. That's the way it works."

Intention is behind everything . . . when it is strong and pure, beautiful things are created.

For the next few hours, even though there was noise and gaiety around him, Josh was struck silent by the depth of the laws Grampa had opened up to him.

· · ·

It was as members of their small middle-school band that Josh and Danny had shared their common interest in music. The friends approached two other school band members to ask them about the idea of forming their own music group. The boys were Colin Guernsey, the band's pianist, and Greg Haycox, who played bass guitar. The four began to meet on weekends in Greg's garage to practice playing some of the easy popular hits of the day. The place contained an old piano and the team would help carry Danny's drum kit there. Like many small groups of budding hopefuls, the boys strove to achieve a sound that pleased their ears. All were talented, but it was Josh's skills that his bandmates recognized, and he became the natural leader.

On a hot Sunday afternoon, the group had been practicing for several hours, going over an arrangement Josh had made of "All You Need Is Love." Josh had been critical of Colin's backing of his solo. As the group continued to practice, he became testier. Finally, when Josh called another stop and announced, "Let's go from the top again," Greg protested.

"No way!" he yelled. "It's plenty good enough. I say we go on to another song."

"We're staying with this one until it's right!" Josh returned loudly.

"You're too picky!"

Danny intervened. "Okay, okay, guys. Calm down. This isn't serious. Yes, Josh is picky. It's because he wants it right. But Josh, Greg's also right. We've been on this too long. Let's move on."

Danny had a way of getting through to Josh, and another piece had been chosen. But the scene sowed the seeds for future episodes of irrational perfectionism and impatient outbursts.

As the next lesson with the Maestro ended, Mr. C said, "Your mother told me you are free this Saturday afternoon. I have two tickets to the Seattle Symphony and I would like you to go with me."

Josh was taken by surprise. He quickly searched his mind for some excuse not to attend, but in the end complied. As the week drew to a close, his mind fussed repeatedly. *How will I get through this? What do I have to do with a bunch of over-cultured geeks? It isn't my scene at all.*

Josh knew his mother had conspired with the Maestro

in this, and he'd stormed and shouted at her, but she calmly said, "It's what your teacher wants." At the appointed time, dressed in his hand-me-down suit and tie, Josh climbed into the Maestro's car and was taken into the city for the dreaded concert. They parked, and Josh felt his feet dragging as they made their way into formidable Benaroya Hall, home of one of the top symphonic organizations in the country.

As they entered the luxurious auditorium, Josh stared around the vast hall and up at the faraway ceiling. They found their seats and he gazed in awe at the orchestra spread before him, preparing to play. Its shining brass and gleaming stringed instruments seemed too much for his eyes to take in. But what most absorbed him were the sounds coming from the group as they tuned. Their instruments, focusing on the G with which the first selection would begin, captivated him. The steady drone, matched by so many kinds of instruments, reverberated through his consciousness.

Applause rose as a distinguished-looking man walked from the wings and took his place facing the orchestra. On a signal from him, all the players' instruments rose in place. There was a momentary rapt silence and then began the first movement of Brahms's Symphony No. 1. Josh had never thought he would hear such music. He was swept away by the processional opening section featuring syncopated rhythms with timpani drums pulsating behind woodwinds and pizzicato strings playing with thematic phrases, finally followed by melodic introductions sung by oboe, flute, and cello.

When a pause came, Josh, enraptured, started to clap, then found himself held back by the audience's expectant silence. The second movement began abruptly, and soon the main theme was being sung stridently by the violins. The brilliant melody brought tears to Josh's eyes; he found himself helplessly in the arms of a musical experience that was beyond what he knew. The repeating theme found a ready answer in the song already pulsing through his soul.

On the drive back after the concert, Josh was excited. "I can't believe how they worked together. I know they must all be the best players and that the—what do you call the guy who wrote it—"

"The composer, Brahms," Peter Colesworthy answered.

"Yeah, Brahms. I knew he must have been a genius. But it was how they put it all together. That band leader . . . "

"Conductor."

"Right, the conductor. He was, well, just the finest. What a lot of work, what a lot of discipline it must take for that many people to be able to perform together like that. Thank you, Mr. C, for taking me. I will never forget this."

"I hope not, Josh. It was my pleasure." As Peter Coleswor-thy drove home after dropping off his young charge, he congratulated himself on having contributed to Josh's musi-cal knowledge. He had imagined the boy would be deeply stirred by the experience, and he had been right.

What Josh's teacher did not know was that the concert had fed into another side of the boy that was deep-seated. The near-perfect musical performance he had witnessed made him say to himself, *I could never be anywhere near as good as any of the people in that orchestra. I don't know why I even try. I'll never be any good.*

Success is not the key to happiness.
Happiness is the key to success. If you love
what you are doing, you will be successful.

—*Albert Schweitzer*

CHAPTER 3

EARLY TREMORS

ONE DAY WHEN JOSH WAS seven, he was in his grandfather's shop watching as the old craftsman shaped the face of a guitar from a piece of bird's-eye maple. He would place the board in a vise, make a few careful strokes with a plane, then remove it and, holding it up, sight the surface for evenness.

"How do you know what each instrument is going to look like when you're finished, Grampa?" Josh asked. "I mean, you make so many different instruments, and each one has a different shape, tone, and feel."

His eyes still fixed on his refinements, Grampa replied, "I guess I get a vision in my mind of how the end result should look, and I simply work to shape each instrument toward that image. It's a patient process of development, mostly by removing pieces that don't fit the image, and finally the true instrument emerges. Then, it's sanding and smoothing the bodies by following the natural wood grain. Eventually, I apply a nice clear coat to bring out the unique shine in each special instrument. Protects it, too."

"Okay," Josh replied, knowing Grampa was seriously downplaying his skills. "But why do you keep looking along the board like that, Grampa?"

"I'm trueing it up," said the old man. "Making sure it's smooth and right." He set the wood once more in the vise and planed it carefully. "It's the same way God does with us, Josh," he said.

"What do you mean?"

"Well, God wants our lives to be sparkling and clean, and He has set His voice within us to keep us true to ourselves as His children. It's called our conscience."

He has set His voice within us to keep us true to ourselves as His children.

Josh thought about that. Then he said, "I have a question, Grampa."

"Always like it when you do," the senior said.

"Can I talk with God?"

Grampa laid the plane aside. Taking the boy by the hand, he led him over to a bench and had them sit down.

"First of all," he said, "I'm very glad you're thinking about that. There's no more important question you could ask." He paused a moment. "But before I answer, let me ask *you* a question. What do you like about the times when you and I talk together?"

"It's my favorite time!"

"Why so?"

"I like the way you listen to me."

"How do you know I'm listening?"

"I watch your mouth when I'm talking. Your lips move and make the same words I say."

Grampa chuckled. "I didn't know I do that. So, one thing you like is you feel listened to. Good. What else?"

"I feel like I can tell you anything, Grampa. I like it that you know me so well."

"Okay, so there's another point. You like being known. Anything else?"

"Well, I like getting to know you, too. When we talk, I find out new things about you, and . . ."

Grampa waited. "What?"

"The more I know about you, the more I love you."

Brynmor Lynk laid his hand gently on Josh's shoulder. "I couldn't have formed a better answer to your question."

"You mean the one I asked about God? But those are things I like about the way *you and I* talk."

"Right. And talking with God is just like that. First, you can tell Him anything. Second, He listens to everything you tell Him."

Josh giggled. "Does His mouth move?"

Grampa smiled. "You could try to find out. Anyway, you can have that same feeling about being known. God listens better than anybody and He knows you through and through. He knows the good things you think—and He knows the naughty ones, too." He noticed that Josh frowned at that statement. "And guess what? He always loves you just the same, with all His great heart."

"Why does God love us, Grampa?"

"Because we're His children. I want you to remember that always. And whenever you are bothered by dark thoughts about yourself, just say, 'I am a child of God!' and that will frighten them away."

Josh sat a while. Finally, he said, "Grampa, I'll never be as good friends with God as you are."

"Not yet."

Their senior year of high school, Josh and his bandmates continued to practice faithfully at every opportunity. In their innocence, they were echoing the bubblegum sound popular in the day. Among the few blues and pop tunes they covered by other artists, Josh inserted some of his own two- and three-chord songs with gooey titles like "Wanna Be with You" and "Have to Tell My Heart."

His experience at the symphony proved to have a long-lasting effect on Josh. Inspired by the flawless harmony of effort he had seen in the orchestra so many years ago, he drove his friends to rehearse their arrangements for each song until their synchrony was honed to near perfection. The other band members were agreeable to this concentration because they saw that their leader demanded even more of himself than he did of them. Each of the four, over the months, had developed Josh's playing until it was becoming a craft. As the first year of their rehearsals ended, it was evident that under Josh's exacting leadership, their sound had become smoother and more professional-sounding.

The proof was in the requests coming in for small engagements. One was a school dance, another a benefit, and several were at retirement homes. Greg's parents lined the group up to play one afternoon at their golf club. All these were free of charge, but the boys were only too glad to be performing before live audiences—though they did prefer that their retiree listeners not doze off to sleep when they played! One day, Josh came to rehearsal with a beaming smile. "We got a gig!" he said. "A real, paying one!" The band's excitement was uncontainable. Their dreams were coming true.

The engagement was a Lion's Club dance for family and friends. "Let's do some good, guys," Josh said. His four-bar opening guitar riff was picked up by Danny's steady beat, and the first song, "Lady Be Good," began. The club members and their families had invited groups of friends and the crowd kept growing. Josh alternated a set of traditional show-tune covers they had developed for older audiences with a few pop tunes they preferred. It took the boys a number or two, but the band soon hit its stride, and the dancers and listeners were plainly appreciating the music they were making.

During their second set, Josh noticed a new group arriving, probably freshmen from the nearby college. Among them was a girl who was on the floor continuously as the partner of one or another of the three young men in her party. She had short dark hair and electric hazel eyes, but mostly what drew Josh's attention was the joyousness in her dancing. She also had a way of gifting each partner with the most radiant smile. There was something about those eyes that kept Josh watching for glimpses of them.

The band struck up a cover it was, in a small circle, already known for. When it was time for his solo, Josh found a beautiful melody escaping which seemed somehow to connect with the girl. With the first riff, she looked up at him in quick surprise, as if someone had called her name. But Josh had closed his eyes to better follow the unfolding melodic pathway. He was feeling a familiar sense of wonderment that came at rare moments when an altogether new and different song would begin to build itself from the melody line of the piece the band was playing. *This could have its own lyrics*, he thought. People around the place were looking up, some of the dancers stopping to listen. Josh leaned back, bending some of the notes so they soared.

He wasn't talking; he was listening. He wasn't playing; he was being played.

"Take another, man!" Danny's voice from behind him confirmed that what was being declared through him had only begun. It was a process of announcing itself just in time—each new phrase just out of reach, but suddenly available, and then done with. He wasn't talking; he was listening. He wasn't playing; he was being played. As he ended the last chorus, the whole venue broke into applause. Josh opened his eyes to see all eyes on him, cheers and whistles drowning the place. Looking around for the girl, he glanced down. At the edge of the stage were those luminescent eyes, looking fully up into his. He felt a jolt. So risky it was, to fall into those depths, yet so compelling. The flash of her smile made something go knocking in his chest.

The silence between them lasted for what seemed an eternity. Finally, she said, "I'm Joy." It was too much for Josh. He went to the microphone and said, "Thank you all. Break time. We'll be right back." He walked back to stand by Danny's drum kit, his back to the audience, as he pretended to tune his guitar.

That service-club dance kicked off the band's early local success. Word of mouth spread quickly. The quality of their music was appreciated, and soon a steady string of dates was on the band's calendar. They were permitted to play at clubs around town, as long as the boys didn't imbibe. Often the crowds were noisy in their appreciation, and at such times Josh noticed how his bandmates' excitement grew.

Besides the follow-up dates that the Lion's Club dance had touched off, there was another more lasting result of that evening. Josh and Joy Younger began to seek each other's company more and more. Theirs was a friendship before it was a romance. They were drawn to each other by a mutuality of values. Joy discerned the depths of Josh's heart; the same qualities his grandfather appreciated endeared him to her. Josh found in her a capacity for enjoyment of life, as well as a wisdom unusual in one her age. She also tolerated his impatience and occasional bursts of temper. Joy was a faithful fan; Josh could always look for her loving gaze shining out of the crowd at each of his band's dates.

. . .

"First time in a studio, boys?" the director, Martin Sheehy, asked.

Silence. The four friends were awestruck. They gazed around the recording studio in open-mouthed silence at the equipment, the microphone setup, the engineer behind the glass. The notion that all this professional expertise could and would be devoted to recording the sounds Josh's little rookie band would make was almost too much to take in. Would they do things right? How would they sound?

He managed to answer the coordinator's question. "Uh, yes. Sorry. Yes, sir. My name is Josh and, uh, we were thinking we would record six songs. How long will that take? How many takes will be required—"

"Hold on, Josh," the man said, smiling. The best way is to start with one track and see where we go, okay?"

It took an hour for the instruments to be brought in, set up, microphoned and tested. The friends continued to be in awe. For them, everything was new. The bewildering technology—sophisticated microphones, lighting, etc.—was almost secondary to the mixture of fear and excitement they were feeling. They moved as in a dream.

Once the work got underway, Josh was at his most persnickety. Made nervous by the concentrated environment and afraid of the outcome, he repeatedly stopped the group in the middle of a take to complain about the sound. Sometimes it was, "We're not together!" Other times it was, "You can't just play the bass notes we worked out. You have to do it in sync with me. I can't even hear myself playing here," or, "You've done that riff a hundred times better than that!"

At the third stop Josh called on the second tune, the engineer shook his head and called the director in. Martin came into the room and said, "Boys, I know you're very particular about making this just right. It's something I see all the time. You're not used to recording, and it's a lot of pressure. How about we just go through all the numbers without any stops and you guys go away and listen to it and decide what to do? Otherwise, this is going to cost you too much."

. . .

The Josh Lynk Band was eventually able to cut a CD and send it to several radio disc jockeys. The gigs came in, and after finishing high school the group finally had the opportunity to play outside their hometown. They were finally on the road, living what seemed a dream life. Months of touring followed, during which Josh and Joy became engaged.

The band was gaining a reputation as a band of promise; its repertoire and fan base were growing. But Josh's impatience and insistence on a certain standard were hard on the other players. As time went on, he was annoyed by his perception of the difference between his own deep commitment to excellence in the music and the motivation of the others. During a break one evening, Josh was annoyed to see Greg and Colin laughing with some girls who crowded around the stage. After the show he said to them, "It seems like you guys are just in this for the fun."

"Sure," Greg answered. "What else?"

Josh just shook his head and walked away. Danny had been watching the scene. Ever the peacemaker, he approached his friend. "Josh, you can't expect those guys to feel like you do about the music."

"Why not?"

"Because you're you. You've got much more of a long view of this work than they do."

"I don't want people in my band who're just in it for kicks!" Josh said heatedly.

"Yeah," Danny said, "but where are you gonna find guys who play like they do? They're good, and you know it. Don't think about giving up on all the work we've done together, man. You have to keep them. They're good guys, and really good players. Don't get so bothered if they want to have fun!"

Josh sighed. "You're right, I guess."

. . .

Josh took a month off from touring and he and Joy were married in a small ceremony. They honeymooned at the lake, swam and paddled, and climbed Ap Jack. Before he knew it, Josh was in a distant city, playing every night and calling home every day.

As time went on, the road was taking its toll. Joy was taking courses toward a nursing degree and couldn't travel with him, and Josh was lonely without her. The business of developing engagements was difficult. He was not only the band's guitarist but most of the time its booking agent, driver, and tour manager. He began to lose track of the cities they visited.

One dark winter afternoon in New Jersey when he and Danny were trudging through the snow, Josh was suddenly seized with the self-doubt that had haunted him those early years, the constant wondering, *Do I have what it takes?* So many times, he'd been tempted to give up. Bad reviews, unresponsive crowds, boredom with fringe-level gigs. *How long will I be doing this? What else should I be doing, if this isn't it?*

At such times, when depression haunted him, Danny recognized what his silence meant, and waited Josh's moods out. Other times he mentored Josh in the rules of common decency, which he knew so well. "Just be nice to everyone, dude," Danny would say. "The promoter, the sound guy, the guy buying the band's CD or shirt at the door, the driver, even your bass player! If it wasn't for every single one of these people, you'd be back home just wishing you could be out here like we are right now. Like it or not, we are a team—our own little traveling community. To be a really great band, we all just have to be excellent to one another!"

It had been a difficult two years since Josh and his young wife's daughter Beth was born with cystic fibrosis. The couple had been overjoyed when Joy became pregnant; Josh had looked forward to being a father, with great resolve to be a better dad than his own father had been. But when the announcement came that the infant had the disease, their hopes seemed shattered.

"Oh Josh, was this my fault?" Joy said through her tears.

Holding his wife's hand in her hospital room, Josh had shaken his head. "Don't even think that, honey," he said. "Grampa used to tell me: 'Remember to see everything that happens, good or bad, as being God's best.'"

They met with a specialist in childhood diseases. After explaining the nature of the malady, he told them that although no cure had been found, advances were being made in the treatment of Beth's syndrome. He then referred the new parents to the hospital's financial counselor.

The woman's manner was kind, but she told them, "I have to be frank with you. This is a disease that brings a large financial burden with it. Not only that, it requires more intensive treatments as the disease progresses, which means increasing time commitments, and larger expenses. You can expect the cost to run at least fifteen thousand dollars per year to start." At home, Josh and Joy pondered the problem. "I just have to work more," Josh said, "and get better-paying jobs."

Cystic fibrosis meant a constant danger of Beth's lungs filling with fluid. Despite the couple's need to support each other in their parenting of their child, Joy would be virtually alone in her caregiving. Between administering medications and keeping airways free, treating little Beth's respiratory issues would require at least two hours of dedicated care per day.

Josh's dilemma was that he wanted to be home now more than ever, but needed to be increasingly busy with performing. His time and efforts on the road were driven not only by an artistic purpose, but also by a deep need to provide for his child. His efforts at securing better venues and better-paying jobs were unceasing.

Beth was a delightful child. From infancy, she possessed an unusually serene nature. Even when she was racked with coughs and wheezing and desperately trying to catch her breath, the little girl would smile reassuringly at her mother. Her inner peace and joy was noticed by all who saw her. Many declared that she seemed like an angel.

Be careful what you set your heart upon—
for it will surely be yours.

—*James A. Baldwin*

CHAPTER 4

THE LURE

THERE WAS A DIFFERENCE in Josh's playing when he returned to the road. People noticed it, and those close to him knew it was because of his new status as a father and provider. He had always been focused; now he was driven to seek some elusive sound or melody. As a result, his ear was sharpening, his creative juices flowing. Sometimes even a few select notes from his guitar would make his bandmates smile and nod their heads, or cause a low "Yeah!" of appreciation from someone in the audience.

His creative fervor was picked up by the other three and reflected in their playing. Fans of the Josh Lynk Band were looking for such quality in the music world, and they praised it when they found it. Seasoned listeners and musicians appreciated finding music in the Josh Lynk Band— now often referred to as the JLB—that was original and always new in some way. They had seen plenty of musicians and groups that were technically good, but who had no heart or "soul" in their playing.

There were times that Josh's ego and conscience were at war. At such times, in the early years, Grampa's face would loom. *But I want it*, would come the inner little-kid thought. And more often than not, the ego won out over his conscience. Looking back later, the truth would always emerge and Josh would see how he had hurt himself and hurt others with his overly perfectionist tendencies and insensitive outbreaks. Then the blackness would descend upon Josh, cloaking him with depression, both inside and out.

Danny knew these moods of his so well. Once, when they were driving and Josh was in the depths, complaining about everything—Colin's keyboard playing, the way the band sounded, the boring tunes, the low-paying gigs that went nowhere, on and on—Danny listened to it all and then he said, "I heard something the other day that's like a riddle. Want to hear it?" No response. "Okay, it goes like this: how do you drive darkness out of a dark room?"

Silence. He figured Josh knew the answer, but he said, "Think about it, man. You can't fight the dark; you can't hit at it with a broom or vacuum it away. You can't wait it out. It won't go away on its own. But if you just strike a match, instantly the dark is gone, as if it never had been."

You can't fight the dark . . . It won't go away on its own. But if you just strike a match, instantly the dark is gone, as if it never had been.

He thought Josh would just keep driving in silence. But then came: "Yeah, so?"

"So, you can't just keep going over personal struggles and dark memories from your past. You've gotta bring in the light of something new, something good, something hopeful. You . . ."

You can't keep going over past struggles and dark memories. You've gotta bring in the light of something new, something good, something hopeful.

"Okay. I get it. I've been thinking about Shawn Hallowell."

"Who's he?"

"That guy I talked to back in Austin, the promoter. He was excited when he heard us, said he could get us some connections."

"Why didn't you tell me?"

"Never mind. Here. Take my phone. His number's there on my address book. Call him up right now."

. . .

As the JLB began to amass more of a following and garner greater media recognition, Danny, Greg, and Colin relished it all. Curiously, Josh seemed almost oblivious to the attention. He was looking for something, seeming to be on a quest for some elusive dream. His nature was such that he could easily become discouraged. The same sensitivity that blossomed out now and then in his musical creativity could put him in the dumps when results were not immediate.

The Josh Lynk Band continually operated on a shoestring budget. Josh was barely making expenses, putting the band up in cheaper hotels, hardly supporting himself. He often complained to Danny about the low money. Together they dreamed of a day when, instead of struggling from gig to gig to make ends meet, they would be prospering, entertaining thousands of fans. When Josh got behind in bill paying or they had to put themselves up in a low-class motel, Danny would say, "R and F, man; R and F. That's our future!" R and F meant rich and famous.

Joy's mother stayed with Beth so Josh and Joy could enjoy a night out. Driving home through a light snow after dinner at a nice restaurant and a movie, Josh fell silent. Joy had noticed that his spirits were down ever since coming off the road this time. Not one to avoid issues, or to mince words when she was on her way to a search for truth about something, she finally broke the silence. "What's going on, honey?"

"I dunno."

"Come on. Talk to me. You're not yourself. That is, you're being a part of yourself that doesn't do you any good."

"I know."

"Then what is it?"

"Nothing."

"Josh!"

He banged his fist against the steering wheel. "I don't *have* it!" he stormed.

"What do you mean?"

"I mean the band needs great songs and, guess what, I don't have the talent to write them. Besides, all the great songs have already been written." He turned the car into the driveway and turned off the ignition. They sat.

"You said all the good songs have been done. What about 'Talked to an Angel'?"

"Fluke!"

"Fluke, huh? What about 'Could We Ever?' What about 'You're On!'"

"Okay, okay," Josh said. "So I wrote some songs."

Joy put her arms around her husband. "Not just songs. Good songs. And has the place where those songs came from somehow gone away from inside you?"

"No, but I can't get to it now. I try but—ah, what's the use?"

"So, you lose touch with it sometimes. And this is just one of those times, right? Big deal. It's your sensitivity—a part of you I love. I don't just love the productive part. I love your willingness to struggle, to go through these dry periods. Your sensitivity is why I—well, your money is really why I married you, but—"

Josh did as Joy wanted him to. He laughed.

"So, come in the house," she continued. "While you make a fire, I'm going to make your favorite drink, lemonade with cranberry juice and seltzer, and whip up a pot of guacamole from some fresh avocados I bought today. We'll sit by the fire and sip our drinks, eat our goodies, cuddle up, and watch a couple of movies."

One misty night when they finished their show in a new city, Greg said, "The Mountain Peaks are playing across town. Let's go hear them." Taking a cab several blocks to downtown, they found the place, a well-known venue where the bigger bands played. A line of fans, some in cowboy hats and boots, waited outside. They stood in line for twenty minutes to finally reach the door, pay an exorbitant fee, and be admitted into the noisy din of the smoky club and led to a back table. The band was doing a tune called "Nobody Wins." As Josh listened, he recognized the leader's twangy solo. "That's note for note what he did on their album," he told Danny." The guitarist was Foster Peaks, leader of the Mountain Peaks.

During the break, Josh was surprised to see Peaks headed to their table. "Aren't you guys the Josh Lynk Band?" he said, smiling. The boys came to their feet with big grins. Josh and Peaks shook hands, and Josh pulled an empty seat over for him. Peaks had long scraggly hair under his Stetson hat, and he wore makeup and strings of beads. "So, you must be gigging in the area?" he said. Josh nodded. "Whereabouts you playing?"

Conscious of the smallness of their venue, Josh mumbled, "Uh, we're at the Evernote across town."

"Hm," Peaks said. "Don't know it. Anyway, it's good to see you. Want to sit in with us for a song?" Josh looked at his bandmates, who were smiling and nodding to the man. He assented eagerly.

After the break, he mounted the stage with the other members of the featured band. As he plugged his guitar in, Peaks went to the microphone. "We've got a treat, folks. This here is my friend Josh Lynk." After a spatter of applause, Peaks turned and cued the band. Josh was momentarily mesmerized by the blast of the first notes. He felt surrounded by talent, and a bit out of his league with the country-western genre. After he had played rhythm through two rounds of the familiar number, he caught Peaks' nod, indicating that he was up for a guitar solo.

The song pattern was easy. The band's backup was superb, bassist and drummer and keyboard providing a perfect ground, and a tenor man noodling alternately behind for wherever Josh wanted to go. He played the opening guitar riff straight with minor variations. Reaching the bridge, he felt a familiar sense of effortless mastery begin to take over. A door was opening to something amazing. Barely aware of the halo of attention from the quieting crowd, he found himself approaching a capacity in himself he'd learned to call the Place, where the melody was but a musical pathway to a new song. The unstruck music that emerged captured the players behind him, lifting them to a rapt concentration.

Josh never knew what happened, only that when the number ended, there was a din of noise around him and he was being hugged by Peaks and congratulated by the others. In their eyes, he saw respect, marking a brotherhood of true talent. Peaks pulled him to the front of the stage;

grabbing his arm, he lifted it high. "Hey!" he shouted into the mike, "Didn't I tell ya? Josh Lynk, folks!" The applause was thunderous.

Well-wishers crowded around Josh when he returned to his table, including several attractive girls. A young man in a tie-dye T-shirt pushed rudely through and breathed beer-ily in his face. "You wail, man!" he said. "Awesome! I'm Alan Reedy, drummer with Xtreme Irony. Come across the street to the Hilton and catch our act!"

Josh then felt a heavy hand on his shoulder. Turning, he looked into a pudgy face with heavy jowls and lidded eyes. The man standing before him, though of less than medium height, must have weighed close to three hundred pounds. "I want to speak to you," the man's oily-sounding voice said. "Here's my card. My office is in Pinnacle Tower uptown. Come and see me later. I'll be up."

Josh looked at the card; the name was Theodore Gan-try. Stubby fingers took the card from Josh, turned it over and then gave it back. On the other side, Josh read *Tiny G.* He felt a start, an uncontrolled tremor travel through him. Here stood one of the top promoters in the entertainment world. Bestowing a sly wink, the huge man turned and waddled off.

Josh looked at Danny, whose eyebrows were doing an up-and-down dance. Greg and Colin were grinning and nodding excitedly.

. . .

When the Pinnacle door opened at his knock, Josh was surprised to see a tall, youngish-looking woman with an incredible figure standing before him. She was dressed in a robe; her face, which once had surely been extraordinarily beautiful, was heavy with makeup and tinged with something hard. "Come in, Josh," she said, smiling invitingly. *She must be a model,* he thought.

"Yes, come in, Mr. Lynk," Tiny G's voice boomed. Josh entered a glamorously finished suite. He was mesmerized by the sheer height of the Pinnacle Tower penthouse, with full-length windows giving way to a panoramic view of the city unlike any he had ever seen. The host's bulging figure was seated behind a large desk, on which rested a tray with the remains of an enormous meal. Despite his greeting and a plastered-on smile, Josh saw that the man's eyes appeared blank, empty of warmth or feeling. "You did yourself a service coming here, my friend," Tiny said, gesturing to a chair facing the desk. "Have a seat. Sandy, get the young man a drink."

"Oh, just orange juice for me, please," Josh said. He looked around the room, noting the pictures of at least a dozen top bands adorning the walls.

His host chuckled. "Like what you see?" he said. Taking the chair, Josh found himself looking up at the other man. He had been placed, as if in a subservient role. "If so," the man continued, "I have a question for you." He lit a cigarette and inhaled deeply. "How would you like to have your own picture up there with theirs?"

There was a silence as Josh felt that same tingle sweep through him. "Every one of those bands," his host continued, "is a client. I might even say I made some of them. Because you see, my friend, it's all in the bookings. And as you may have guessed, I've asked you here because I would like to be your agent."

Josh sat there, a tide of delight spreading through him. Then he frowned. "You keep talking about me," he said. "You mean you'd be booking the Josh Lynk Band, right?" He waited while Tiny G inhaled deeply and puffed out a smoke ring, seemingly in deep thought.

"No," the man finally said. "I would feature you with one of the most successful bands I handle, replacing the present lead guitarist with whom I've had some issues. You've heard enough about these stars to know that such a move would put you immediately on top of the game. You'd be playing and you'd also be writing songs. Because I've heard some of your songs, and they're good."

Josh felt a numbness spreading through his chest. Moments ago, this had seemed a dream come true. Now he was faced with choosing for himself and betraying his friends. He shook his head. "No, Mister G, I—I just couldn't do that."

Tiny G studied Josh's features. Behind the young man's noble-sounding words, the promoter recognized an ego struggling with greed and wanting to appear principled. He knew how to topple that wall. "Come, come, my friend," he said. "I know you're not only a very gifted musician, but an ambitious one. Think this over. I am offering you nothing less than a major leap in your career. You'll be playing with the best, making top-selling recordings. Your Josh Lynk Band has been opening for other bands," Tiny G went on. "Where you're going with me, you'll be the feature act. And the money, oh, my friend, the money you'll make!"

At the mention of money, the thought came to Josh: *Joy*

and I wouldn't have to worry so much about Beth's care. Not realizing he was rationalizing a decision based on naked desire, he warmed further to the deal he was being offered. He made one last effort of resistance. Rising from his low chair and facing the big man, he declared, "I have to think this over."

"Well, now, that's the thing, Josh." Tiny G said, swiveling his chair to one side and carefully examining his well-manicured fingernails. "My offer is only good while you are here. Once you leave, it is rescinded."

Josh's mind seemed to go blank. He stood there looking around, as if seeking a solution. The clouds outside Pinnacle Tower had descended and were now wringing themselves inside out; each window seemed to sweat as the drum of rainfall became more audible. Josh looked over and found Sandy seated across the room, aiming a meaningless smile at him.

Tiny G slid a sheaf of papers and a pen across the desk toward him. "Here is the contract. It has the handsome salary you would start with, plus your percentages for recording deals and residuals. Even some profit sharing with the bigger events like stadiums and festivals. I advise you to take time to read it through before you sign. Now, if you'll excuse me." The heavy figure pushed itself out of the chair with difficulty and toddled into the next room.

Josh's mind seethed between options. Yes, he could leave—prove himself faithful to the friends with whom he had played and planned for nine years—and continue to struggle! Or he could cut them blindly away and embrace a future of working in the rarefied and privileged atmosphere of stardom. The thought of Beth hovered in the background of his predicament. To have those financial problems so neatly addressed was the only true excuse he needed. *There,* he thought, *that's definitely the reason I should do this.*

When the stout promoter returned to the office, he went to his desk and picked up the contract. His pudgy face beamed when he saw Josh's signature on the document. "Congratulations, Mr. Lynk," he said. "You have made the right choice. You will never be sorry."

Why am I doubting that? Josh wondered. Aloud, he said, "Uh, you spoke of my replacing someone."

A shade fell over the promoter's eyes. "Yes. Hildreth," he mumbled. "Know him?"

"Jack Hildreth? The lead guitarist with Tawna?"

A nod.

"Where's he, uh, going?" Josh wondered.

"Well, for now to Subway Moon. If he isn't careful, he'll be playing in bar-band city. Anyway, you take a week off. I'll let you know where to show up. Here's some mad money." The big man tossed an envelope to Josh as his cell phone buzzed. "I have to take this. I think we're done here, yes?" Tiny G's handshake was moist, without pressure. He swung away, leaning far back in his big chair. "Pepper, my friend! What did you find out?"

Josh went out, feeling faint. *I'm with Tawna?* The splendor and wonder of it was there for a few moments. Then as he stood waiting for the elevator, it was replaced by a crushing black cloud of self-doubt.

. . .

Down in the lobby, he called Joy. "Honey? Did I wake you? Oh, you've been with Beth. How's our angel?"

He waited impatiently through the report. "Ah, hug that sweet little girl for me. Um, I have great news. Your husband is now playing guitar with a little up-and-coming group called Tawna!"

Silence. He waited. "Did you hear me? What do you think? Yes, honey, I know we should have talked, but I had to—Yeah, I know. Nope. I haven't told the guys yet. Yes, okay, we'll talk. I love you." He hung up and walked out of the elegant condominium into darkness and downpour. In the cab back to his hotel, he tried to think through this sudden fast-forwarding of his life's movie.

· · ·

"*What?*" The unbelieving question came from all three band-mates. Their shock and awe at the news was palpable. Their anger and accusations of his betrayal swept over Josh like a flood.

"Why didn't you tell us first, before deciding?" was the question from all of them.

"I should have," Josh said lamely. "I just couldn't, the way he put it."

"Didn't the guy even give you time to evaluate the choice?" Colin said.

"Yeah, and how about giving you your choice of band?" Danny added. "I kind of wish it wasn't Tawna."

"Right," Greg added. "Tawna has a reputation for being

kind of wild and loose. What do you think about being part of a band like that?"

"No one knows for sure because we haven't ever actually been around the band. For all we know, that could all be media hype and rumors to sell the band's persona. Anyway, JLB proved we could have fun, make good music, and be 'good guys.'"

Danny looked thoughtful. "Just be careful," he said. "Stick to your guns, and make us proud. They have no idea what a great guy they're getting."

Josh was humbled. "Look," he said, "you guys know me, and you know I don't care about parties, alcohol, drugs, or women. Even playing in clubs and being around crazy fans, I've always stayed strong and tried to do my very best. I've never sacrificed my personal values. Besides, maybe I can be a good influence on them."

As the morning wore on, he did his best to explain and justify and apologize. Then the noise gradually calmed down and each of the three seemed to retreat into his own thoughts. Greg was first to announce his decision. "Well, I was about to quit anyway. I've had it with the road and this life. My dad runs an insurance company and I've already told him I'm going to work with him."

Colin was next: "I know a guy with a decent outfit that plays near my house. I think I'll go home and jam with them and take it easy."

Last came Danny. He gazed at Josh with a long mourning look. Then he stood, went over to his friend, and motioned for him to rise. Danny was famous for his hugs, and he gave one now. Josh broke down and wept in his arms. "We'll keep up, won't we?" Danny blurted, as he held Josh away and looked into his eyes. "Of course!" Josh said, attempting to chuckle while recovering his composure. "So what's your plan, Dan?"

Danny shrugged. "We'll see. Maybe my job will be watching you wherever you go."

. . .

As he closed the chapter with the JLB and his friends, Josh couldn't help but to look forward to his next stage with anticipation and excitement. Before he knew it, the time had come to join up with his new band. Tiny G had arranged for Josh to catch the first flight out of Seattle.

Had he realized how tightly the door closing behind him would separate him from all he had known, Josh would not have smiled so often—and so helplessly—as he gazed out the window of the airplane.

All you need in this life is ignorance and
confidence, and then success is sure.

—*Mark Twain*

CHAPTER 5

LIVING THE DREAM

A S A BOY, JOSH HAD watched rock concerts on television; he never dreamed he would be a part of them. The few live performances he had attended growing up had fascinated him. He felt the pull of wanting to do what those musicians were doing. His favorite band was Santana, and his hero was the band's Mexican guitarist, Carlos Santana, who was admired throughout the industry not only for his talent but for his humanness. Now, having found himself a member of one of the most promising bands, which had risen to fame the year before, in the back of his mind Josh wondered if Santana had been the inspiration for Tawna's name.

Following his initial rush of wonder and elation at his new status, Josh's self-confidence had taken a plunge. On his first day reporting for rehearsal after a week at home, he could hardly bring himself to leave the cab as it waited before the rehearsal hall in downtown Cincinnati, the band's home base. Entering the studio carrying a case with the Old Warrior guitar Grampa had made for him so long ago, Josh had been battling the doubts and fears that had haunted him ever since his signing on.

The size of the place shocked him; it dwarfed the small rehearsal studios the JLB had used. Josh stood gazing at the arena-scale stage, expansive lighting, and massive sound systems, all contained in a building the size of an airport hangar. A man who was busy getting the sound, lights, and rigging to work together stopped working and came over to him. "You're Josh Lynk," he said. "I'm Paul Timberlake, Tawna's tour manager. Welcome aboard. You guys have a big show in less than a week and I'm making sure your rehearsal space duplicates the stage setup."

Josh gazed around in awe. "I never dreamed the gigs would be so choreographed," he said. As he spoke, a side door opened and five men, obviously musicians, entered the studio. "Here's your band," Timberlake said.

The musicians came over and greeted him. "Hey, man. You gotta be Lynk, right? Tiny said you were coming." Josh was speechless as he recognized the players from public-ity photos. They grouped about him, shaking his hand and offering good-natured warnings about one another. Key-boardist Dylan Terry pointed to an olive-skinned bandmate, saying, "This here's Henry Garcia, our drummer. We call him the Russian Dragon, 'cause he's always either rushin' or draggin' the beat."

Garcia, a bearded man whose thick arms were covered with tattoos, countered with his own jibe. "Yeah, well, you'll find out why we call this guy 'Rolex.' He's a lot of show, but he can't keep time!"

Another musician, lead singer Bill Joist, was introduced as being known for his "crossfade dissonance." Josh looked confused. A red-headed young fellow, whom Josh recognized as bassist Toby Denning, spoke up: "It means his preference for illicit substances and alcohol causes harmonic discord." The verbal sparring went on, obviously well-rehearsed and for the newcomer's benefit.

"So," Jimmy Keno, the saxophone player, said, "you're one of us now. Do you know Jack Hildreth?" At mention of the musician Josh had replaced, the others fell silent. Who was Josh, their looks implied, to be replacing Tawna's featured soloist? Josh shook his head. More silence.

"Sucks how players get popped in and out of bands by this conglomerate," somebody mumbled, to murmurs of agreement.

They stood there. Then Keno said, "Well, are you any good?"

Josh smiled. "I can carry a tune, I guess." That seemed to satisfy them.

"So, plug in your axe and let's play something,"

Bill Joist called for a slow-tempo blues song, a B. B. King number everyone knew, and they were off. Josh knew the opening instrumental riff by heart, and the melody he laid down was backed solidly by the band's tight ensemble— and amplified perfectly by the flawless sound system. Surrounded by excellence, Josh was floating in a dream.

Joist started into a couple of verses:

"Every day I have the blues . . . "

The vocal soon gave way to two rounds of a keyboard solo by Dylan Terry. Josh's exhilaration at Terry's masterful playing was tempered by nervousness; his guitar solo would be next. When Joist looked up at Josh, he tried to relinquish his fears to some higher power and launched into his most critical audition. At first simply and lyrically, then with increasing fervor, he felt his way through two choruses, aware of the others' eyes and ears on him.

Finishing his solo, he was surprised when Joist told him, "Take a couple more," to nods from the others. Relaxing, Josh searched his way deeper into the song's classic twelve-bar chord progression, deeply aware of wanting to do his best. When he ended, there were nods and smiles. *Guess I didn't mess up*, he thought.

. . .

In his next days with the band, because of his self-consciousness and fear of failure, Josh could only see in these men the slick, surface-level, hail-fellow attitude that prevailed. Listening as the players swapped suggestive jokes and stories in a spirit of arrogant bravado, he couldn't sense the goodness that was in each man, which he would in time come to know.

Everywhere he looked, easy money spoke. Drugs, money, liquor, and aggressive women were not only available, it seemed to Josh they were everywhere. Meals were sumptuous. Hotel accommodations were the plushest suites. The faces of two of the best-known players were lit with an oily glow, the mark of a surfeit of sensual pleasure. Though no one was more than thirty years old, hard living already showed in their lined features. As he continued to find no respite from the conspicuous lifestyle that surrounded him, Josh often wondered if he had made the right choice. *I didn't sign up for this part of the deal*, he would reflect silently. *I wish Joy could be here more often.* Josh found himself missing the simplicity and sincerity of his old life.

I didn't sign up for this part of the deal . . . I wish Joy could be here more often.

There was one exception among his new bandmates. Josh felt himself drawn most to Toby Denning, the red-headed young bass player. *This is a friend*, he thought, *someone on my own wave length.* The next day when he walked into the studio, he found Denning alone, engrossed in tuning a new Fender Stratocaster.

"Nice guitar," Josh ventured.

Denning looked up and smiled. Without a hint of sarcasm, he said, "So, have you come to lift our struggling band to its next level?"

"I guess," Josh replied, smiling. "Hey, I like your bass work. You lay down such a solid groove behind us."

"Thanks. I do some arranging and writing, too, as well as keeping all the basses and guitars up."

Josh paused, uncertain about bringing up a sensitive subject with his new friend. He decided to go ahead. "Hey, what happened to Jack Hildreth, anyway? He was a major talent. Why did they let him go?"

"Didn't Tiny tell you?" Toby queried.

Josh shook his head, feeling he shouldn't have asked. "Well, it was a surprise to the rest of us. Tiny's unpredictable like that." Toby gestured to the guitar he was holding. "Ever see a brand-new Strat?"

Josh shook his head. "Only one I ever saw was in a music store."

"Well, guess what," Toby said, walking over to Josh with the guitar. He lifted the broad strap over Josh's head, and Josh felt the weight of the storied instrument as it hung in front of him. "It's yours."

"Wait! Mine?"

Toby nodded. "Tiny G's compliments."

"But a new Strat? I never dreamed . . ."

"Hey, you didn't think you were gonna play with Tawna using that beat-up axe you dragged in, did you?"

Josh had a momentary reaction to Toby's slur on the guitar Grampa had made for him, the old friend he had played and carried to every job, the symbol of where he had come from that had served him so well all these years. But he forgot it when Toby reached over and plugged the new guitar's cord into an amplifier. "How 'bout a test drive?" Toby said. The weight of the gleaming new instrument, the coolness of its surface in Josh's hands, swept away all other considerations. Slipping on a thumb pick, he launched into a ten-second blues arpeggio that widened Toby's eyes.

Toby smiled his appreciation of Josh's talent. "So, now you're a god," he said.

Josh took the guitar off and laid it down. "Thanks," he said. "I'll be back." He made for the door, took the elevator to the street, and walked out into the autumn sunshine. Crossing the street to a park, he began walking through the lush green space. A mother was playing with her young boy. Squirrels were chasing each other up and down a tree. A runner came toward him and smiled as she flashed by.

His mind was in a commotion. The old darkness was creeping in again, the low feeling that paralyzed him whenever someone recognized what was in him. The self-distrust was threatening to wipe out the admiration that had come from Toby, and from receiving the new guitar. This time, however, something was different. A kind of prayer came to him.

Grampa, is this you? You are the one who always told me to think better of myself. Is this what you meant, because it's too much! I can't contain it. I did feel like a god, just for a moment, back there when Toby said it. But it's not a boasting, selfish feeling. It's like a new suit I'm trying on to see if it fits me. Is this who you always said I was? I don't know how long I'll feel this way, but thank you, Grampa! I love you.

As a lightness and blissful feeling permeated his body, he suddenly stopped. He was remembering what Grampa told him to do when the darkness came. It was to stop and say, "I am a child of God." *That's what I'm feeling, isn't it, Grampa? I didn't even need to say it. It just came to me.*

For an hour he walked, relishing the moments, loving everything and everybody he saw.

· · ·

In keeping with the band's culture of fun-making, Josh's bandmates began to call him "Shu." The naming started when Bill Joist reminded the group, "Our friend Josh has a storied name. You may remember that after the Jews wandered in the desert for forty years, it was Joshua who led them into the Promised Land. Maybe our own Joshua here is destined to lead us into the promised land of riches and plenty. Huh?" The others cheered. "But Joshua is kind of formal, don't you think? So"—turning to Josh, Bill placed his hand on his shoulder—"I dub thee Shu, short for Shua, short for Joshua!"

After that, whenever Josh heard the designation Shu, he felt a gladness. He had been initiated. Also, in the days that followed, Josh came to appreciate Toby Denning's friendship more and more. Toby was known as the "good cop" of Tawna's ensemble. In contrast to the other high-profile members, whose wild escapades were frequently reviewed in fan magazines, Toby was quiet and unassuming. For that reason, he was usually placed in the forefront when the band's better face was to be displayed, such as for interviews and publicity events.

It was their love of the music that united Josh and Toby. To Josh, his new friend's songs, with their lyrics marked by a certain purity of feeling, were the standouts of Tawna's repertoire.

Josh came awake as the bus pulled into the downtown Denver station. Exhausted from the previous night's concert in Minneapolis, he had slept through the trip. A limousine with the Tawna leopard logo on its side was waiting to convey the band the ten miles to Red Rocks—the huge outdoor theater where they were to play. As they departed the luxe car, their ears were assaulted by the cheers of fans who were lined up at the entrance to the venue. Josh was surprised to see the size of the crowd that had gathered so early; the band's setup would take another three hours.

They entered the famous open-air amphitheater and Josh saw the large disc-shaped rock that tilted from behind the stage, and another huge vertical rock angled outward from stage right, along with several large outcrops, all a rusty red color. "How many seats does this place hold?" he asked one of the ushers accompanying the band to the stage. "Nine-thousand, five-hundred and twenty-five," came the answer. The man added, "You'll appreciate the perfect acoustics."

Later, when the concert was ready to begin and he looked out at the huge crowd filling the stadium, Josh was taken aback by the band's distance from the concertgoers. The nearest fans seemed miles away, behind rows of monitors, security guards, and safety fences. Most of them would be watching the action on the enormous screens mounted on either side of the stage. *They might as well have stayed home and watched a concert video*, he thought.

The very things that had made Tawna special—the urgency, the immediacy, the personality—were completely lost when they played a large venue like this. When Bill Joist opened the event by yelling, "Good evening, Denver! how ya doin'?" Josh was embarrassed by the counterfeit intimacy. Even the roar of the crowd felt like a meaningless, practiced response.

As the band launched into the first number, Josh was astonished to see that his fellow musicians were doing their part to push their listeners as far away as they could. They were strutting about, turning their backs on the audience. *These guys don't want to feel like normal dudes*, he told himself. *They want to feel like rock gods.* As the evening wore on, he had the feeling that the screaming admirers out there in the sea of seats expected to be treated this way, and actually enjoyed it. It wasn't the music they bought tickets for—it was this blatantly irreverent show, in which the band was performing for itself.

· · ·

In his embrace of the move from minor- to major-league status, Josh never dreamed that he would miss the closeness and intimacy with fans he enjoyed when playing smaller venues. Now he was remembering the feelings of affection and respect that were always present in the dimly lit dives and intimate clubs his band had played through the years. The fans were right there, a few yards away, and their appreciation buoyed the musicians' performance. Now, when he had worked hard in rehearsals to be ready to give his best performance with his new band, he could gain no sense of genuine appreciation from the raucous crowd. Tawna's removal from their audience made the whole performance seem unreal.

The band performed a career-spanning fifteen-song set list. After the concert ended, Josh was packing his guitar into its case, to be gathered up by the road crew. His brain was reeling from the hours of deafening racket when he saw a tiny envelope taped to the inside pocket of the guitar case. Removing a small card from it, he read:

Just be yourself. Everyone else is already taken. Remember, I am with you always.

— Joy

Tears came to his eyes. It was as if Joy had been there in the amphitheater as he had played. He felt a flood of love and something he had come to call the Grampa Connection. Standing there, he reveled in it, so different from the cold, unfeeling environment he had just been engrossed in.

. . .

By now Joy was pregnant with their second child, and although he phoned regularly, Josh was becoming a stranger at home. One night he returned home late from a long road stint; the next morning, he was sitting with Joy when five-year-old Beth came in the room to ask her mother something.

"Hey," Joy said, "can't you say hi to your daddy?"

"Oh hi, Daddy," the tot said. "Have you been gone?"

The day before Josh was to leave for a six-week-long period, he was playing dolls on the living room floor with his daughter. In the manner of innocent wisdom that characterized her, Beth looked at him and said, "Daddy, do you like to play music?"

"Sure," Josh said enthusiastically. "I love it. Why do you ask me?"

"Well, the other night Mommy and I were watching you on TV playing with your band and you didn't look happy."

The high-flying economy of the music industry bewildered Josh. Instead of struggling from gig to gig to make ends meet, the amount of money a band made was linked to the infrastructure surrounding a particular venue. Everything depended on an act's ability to attract paying fans. The musicians were paid a flat rate for a certain number of tour dates.

One day, Josh overheard Tiny G telling someone about his troubles arranging a stadium tour for the band. "If you could sell the full twenty thousand tickets and fill the lawn for this gig, our earning potential would be off the charts. But we're talking about Roguesville, a town where we'll likely fill around ten thousand seats. Figure it out, my friend. We're not making that much more by going to a stadium than we are by going to the fine arts downtown that has a three-thousand-person capacity." Josh marveled at how rapidly his manager made decisions based on juggling the profit margins expected from different towns and venues.

Although their tour manager kept a tight schedule for the band, as with all touring musicians, the Tawna bandsmen had many hours when they were not rehearsing or performing. Traveling and waiting on the bus or in hotel rooms for their next move bored them. Consequently, they would amuse themselves by smoking, drinking, telling stories, and playing poker. Josh mostly tried to keep to himself. By now, he had begun to wonder about signing the contract with Tiny and joining Tawna. The roughness of his bandmates' lifestyle, except Toby, had many times made him question his decision. *I told Danny and the guys I could keep my own counsel with this crowd, but it's honestly not very easy.*

Composing had always been an interest of Josh's. He spent many hours poring over notebooks, longing to contribute a song to the band's repertoire. In the past the ideas were simple and clean; nowadays, with the influence of his band and the big crowds, it was harder to capture such sweetness. The music was rougher, bolder, and the genre didn't suit his temperament. Was it love he wanted to write about? Loneliness? Freedom? Friendship? Desire? The sheets stayed blank, with mere scribbles around the edges.

When the holidays came, Josh learned that Tawna was booked to play a "secret" Christmas show, a benefit for a homeless charity, at a small club. The bandsmen looked forward to the gig; it was a rare opportunity to reunite them with their fans. Although their egos relished being arena-filling headliners, they knew it was in the dimly lit dives and intimate clubs that they made their most exciting live music. Walking to the club where they were to play and looking at the Christmas tree lights glowing from windows, Josh and Toby talked about home.

"Guess it's tough being away from your family," Toby said.

"Really. My little girl is probably looking at her own tree lights just now."

They reached the venue and went to the stage to set up. After all the big shows the band had been playing, Josh was glad to be back in a small downtown club. It was a more intimate setting, not only with the audience, but with the band members as well. On the large stages, they were often separated from one another—together, yet alone.

As they played the first number, it was evident that all the musicians were happy. The fans were eager; they listened with appreciation, many of them mouthing the words Bill Joist sang. There was a sense of exultation that spread through the place, uniting musicians and listeners. As the players looked at one another, their eyes glowed, as if they were saying, *We've never sounded better*. Afterward, packing up, the men in the band wished each other a merry Christmas, but they had already blessed one another with their songs.

· · ·

In the months that followed, Josh would come to know each of his bandmates intimately. Playing with them, traveling with them, living with them, he knew their strengths and their weaknesses. He saw them happy and sad, angry and helpless, drunk and asleep, elated with fame and made fools of by women. And in their creative moments, he would see the virtuoso in each man. They would argue and hate one another, go apart and come together, but they were, despite their distractions, a team. Their mutual love of music making aggregated their talents. It was the one uniting stream that made them the band they were.

I am as bad as the worst, but,
thank God, I am as good as the best.

—*Walt Whitman*

CHAPTER 6

CORPORATE!

DESPITE THE JOKES ABOUT BILL Joist's predilection for recreational substances, Josh was drawn to the singer. Joist's sense of humor was always in play. It seemed he had hilarious comments to contribute to every situation. Bill was especially clever in his ability to bring out the absurd side of serious matters. Once he designed a Tawna T-shirt, which sold widely. The front showed the band's traditional logo, a growling leopard's face. On the back was the following:

> *Bad music*
>
> *Overpriced albums*
>
> *Rip-off concerts*
>
> *Nasty, dirty musicians*

Though Bill and Josh were frequently together and Josh assumed Bill used drugs, he could never quite tell if, or when, his friend was under the influence. He asked Bill's best friend, Jimmy Keno, about it, figuring Jimmy knew Bill best and could give him the straight scoop.

"He's always high," Keno said. "He's just got loads of tolerance."

Josh gave an uncomfortable chuckle. He lacked the personal experience to fully appreciate Jimmy's offhand comment, but he knew he felt uneasy with this incredibly casual attitude toward drugs. Not knowing how to express his distaste, he kept silent. But the silence made him feel even more uncomfortable.

. . .

The band finished a big concert in Albuquerque, then had a layover day in town—a rare day off. The band members sat, bored and restless, around the common room of their suite until evening came. Josh was working on a letter to his children. Suddenly Henry said, "This doing nothing blows! I say we all hustle downtown and have ourselves a little, shall we say, outing?" There was immediate agreement and all prepared to leave. Aware of the drinking and carousing that would inevitably occur, Josh held back.

"S'matter, Shu?" Dylan said jeeringly. "Don't want to hang out with your dissipated brethren?"

"Yeah, Shu," the others joined in. "You too good for us?"

"No way," Josh said, getting up. "Where we going?"

Contrary to Josh's expectation of starting with dinner, the group's immediate destination was a bar. Then a second bar, and then a third. Josh concluded early on that dinner would come later, if at all; his friends were busy demonstrating the fine art of barhopping. As hours passed, he lost track of how many saloons they had visited. All but he and Toby were soon in various stages of intoxication. A good deal of whiskey had softened the firm lines of some faces and a few voices were slurred.

As a number of young women began to be added to the entourage, certain traits in the men, facilitated by alcohol, began to emerge. Bill tried to be entertaining. Henry became loving and sentimental. Dylan withdrew into sadness. Jimmy became belligerent. As the night drew on, Josh was hoping against catastrophe, but such was inevitable. In the largest, most crowded tavern of all, one of Joist's witty remarks caught Toby's fancy, and he started laughing uproariously. A burly man, who was watching Toby breaking up, came and stood in front of him with his hands on his hips. "Hey," he said. "What you got to be so happy about?"

An immediate silence was broken by Bill Joist's voice: "Hey, what you got to be so sad about?" The belligerent stranger, along with two other toughs, turned on Bill, and suddenly the whole place erupted in chaos. Josh couldn't believe how fast it happened. It was as if everything was staged, primed, and awaiting that first altercation. Yells and screams split the air. Fists and bottles flew. Josh was shoved to the floor and a heavy boot came down on his hand. Wincing in pain as he arose, he sought out Toby, who was also looking for him. "Let's get out of here!" they both said.

. . .

The next morning Josh phoned home. "Sorry I didn't call last night, honey," he said. "We had a little incident."

"Hm. What was that?"

Josh related the evening's events.

"Well," Joy said, "I guess it comes down to the company you keep."

"I guess it does, and I don't feel very good about being part of it."

"I know," said Joy. "You're not a guy who'd get himself into a bar fight without considerable help."

"And that's just what I had."

"Right." Joy paused. "Do you remember what you told me Grampa said about this?"

"Uh, no." Josh was always surprised when Joy recalled the words of his grandfather. It was as if she'd been there to hear them herself.

"He was talking about how strongly the influence of companions can be," she said, "and he told you, 'Your environment is often stronger than your willpower.'"

"It certainly was this time," Josh said sheepishly.

"Josh," Joy persisted, "please try to be more careful out there. I know your heart is in the right place, but that's not enough to keep you out of harm's way. You have to make the right decisions, too."

Josh exhaled a lengthy sigh. "I know, honey," he said. "Thanks for reminding me. I sure wish you could be here right now. I miss you so much."

As he hung up, he acknowledged to himself how much he had strayed from his spiritual element. *Okay, so I got myself in trouble by who I hung out with. But I wasn't the wrong-doer.* Aware of his inner doubletalk, he added, *Gotta keep better watch on who I play with.* He thought about Grampa. *What a long time it's been since I've heard his voice.* He was about to dial Grampa's number when another thought came: *This is not a great time. Last night wasn't my fault but, like Joy said, it happened to me because of who I was hanging out with. I couldn't stand for Grampa to be ashamed of me.* He put the cell phone back in his pocket.

The phrase "new album" had been gaining whispered momentum among Tawna members. Jimmy Keno seemed to be the source of the rumor, so Josh asked him about it. "Yeah," said the reed man. "In its infinite wisdom, corporate has decreed that we need to cut a new album, then spend a year promoting it all over creation."

"You don't sound very happy about it," Josh ventured. He knew that, had the speaker been one of his old JLB buddies, there would have been huge excitement behind the announcement.

"Can't say that I am," his friend said. "It's a ton of work. And who's to say the songs will be any good, or that the fans will like them?"

"I know," Josh said, "but it's fun to get into new stuff. And maybe the album will be a big hit. I think the recording and album-making process sounds great."

"That's a good attitude to have," Jimmy said, "in the face of what's actually behind all this. Which is a relentless, cold-hearted, and conscienceless industrial machine that demands periodic feeding in the form of sales." Josh thought about that. "By the way," Jimmy added, "have you noticed some strange-looking dudes in the vicinity?"

"Yeah, now that you mention it." Josh had seen two or three men, dressed in jeans and tees like the band members themselves, dropping in and out of the band's workspaces without notice.

"Corporate!" Jimmy said, his eyes rolling.

Despite Keno's disheartening pronouncement, the band-mates were engaged in the process. From past experience, they knew that good songs—at least some good ones—would come out of the process. And they would be glad to be off the road. Soon the official word came down. There would be no more touring. The band would focus on writing new material and recording it in the studio.

One day, Toby said to Josh, "Let's go to lunch."

"Sure," Josh said, glad for the invitation.

Soon the two were seated in a booth in a nearby restaurant. After they ordered meals, Josh said, "So, it's time for writing songs."

"Yep."

"I wanted to ask you how you see this song writing is to be done."

"You know, you're a songwriter," Toby assured him. "Writing a song is always essentially the same thing; it's a trial-and-error process, backing and filling, with revisions and restarts. Ideas you've messed around with and have set aside are brought out and looked at."

"Yeah," said Josh. "It does sound the same. Hey, I've gotta tell you, the songs you wrote for the band have always been great."

Toby shook his head. "Yeah, well, that was then. It's far more mechanized now. Corporate's breathing down our necks. Songs aren't really songs anymore, they're just tracks, like piece-parts of an album. And the tracks they want are tuned to the latest sizzle—what's selling out there. You know how perceptive the public is."

"Yeah," Josh said. "It's just a lot of noise these days."

The two sat picking at their food for a while. Then they both said simultaneously: "Hey, I've got—" Then they burst out laughing. "You go," Josh said.

"Okay," Toby said excitedly, "I thought we—you and I— could take a run at knocking out a song together!"

Josh brought his palms together in a loud clap. "Exactly my thought!"

Josh had gained many new friends during his time with the band. Besides his fellow musicians, there was the road crew. The group included managers, production leaders, front-of-house and monitor engineers, lighting directors, technicians for each instrument and band member, pyro-technic crew, personal security, truck drivers, and merchan-dise personnel. Local crews would supplement this core team in each town, powering the setup and teardown pro-cesses as well as providing auxiliary staff for food, merchan-dise, and backstage operations.

Josh had become friends with Owen Crump, a hard-working roadie nearly twice his age. Owen was a top drum

We're keeping an ear out for news regarding the upcoming album release from superband, Tawna. Latest industry reports say that mega-corporation CEA has assigned writing teams to help the poor, struggling Tawna composers. Do bandies Keno and Joist—the pair who've come up with solid hits like "You Never" and "Daddy Knows"—now need their hands held? We've also heard rumors of horns and backup singers being added for the new product, but it remains to be seen whether such ear candy will result in better songs. Maybe it will be with Tawna as with Beckwith Blues and Transgarden (if you can recall those bands): a pair of really fine song collections, followed by a meager string of soundalikes. Will the Jaws 3 syndrome apply here?

—Cincinnati Times-Telegraph

technician whom Josh had met soon after joining the band. Owen was from Liverpool, and Josh liked the stories he told about being a musician during the so-called British Invasion. Owen's accent generated much kidding from the players: "Hey, Owen, were you the drummer before Ringo?" etc. Owen always had a comeback, though: "Yeah, and the lads told me many times they regretted letting me go!"

Owen was a true fan of Josh's solos. His usual remark after hearing a solo by his friend was, "Wizard!" One evening, Josh found his friend looking tired after his day's work. "You look beat," Josh said.

Owen sighed. "I'm knackered."

"I'm on my way to the practice room," Josh said. "What say you come along and give me feedback on some new riffs I'm working on?"

"Cracking!" Owen exclaimed.

In the practice room, Owen sat down and watched as Josh warmed up the keyboard and plugged his guitar into an amp. Setting the drum machine to a medium bass and hi-hat beat, he started to rumble out some low notes, just free-forming. Occasionally a smile would flicker across Owen's face, showing his appreciation for what Josh was creating. As he played, Josh experimented, having no set plan. After a while he forgot Owen and, secure in his element, he looked for a certain connection. It was then that a scene flashed in his mind. It had been a long time since he'd thought of Grampa, but somehow the moment prompted this memory.

It was after Grampa had given Josh the guitar he'd made for his birthday. Josh had been practicing with it and this day he brought the guitar to his grandfather's shop. He was showing the old man some original riffs he had been working out. When he paused, Grampa nodded and said, "Tell me, Josh, where do you get your ideas?"

Josh shrugged and said, "Oh, they just come to me."

"How do they come to you?" Grampa said earnestly. "Can you tell me just what it feels like for you? You are playing and something happens, like it did just then. So, tell me."

Josh thought a moment. "Well, it's a little like it isn't even me playing." He heard a release of breath from Grampa. "I just listen and follow along."

The old man's face was beaming. "I thought so!" he exclaimed. "You are journeying in your music, boy! You're an example of something Picasso once said: 'Inspiration exists, but it must find you working.'"

Inspiration exists, but it must find you working.
—Pablo Picasso

There in the practice room with Owen, that sudden memory connected Josh; he was playing the same way he'd played for Grampa so long ago. When the realization came, a new level of inner listening was turned on. The sound of his guitar became mesmerizing for him. He didn't need to know where the music was taking him—he simply followed. On and on it went, leading him.

Suddenly he stopped, grabbed a notebook, and began scribbling notes on a blank page.

Owen remained silent, knowing his friend was capturing something he had played on a lead sheet. Finally, Josh looked up, his face lit with a strange innocence. He said, "There was a particular set of notes that grabbed me."

"I think I may know right when it happened. Play it for me, will you, mate?"

Josh played the four-bar line.

Owen jumped up. "Smashing! That was it!"

Josh laughed. "Is that good?"

"It's amazing! You and I recognized the same line. It's gorgeous, mate! You've got to do more with it."

Josh was pleased to know that Owen's response echoed his own. He took it as a statement of faith. "Yeah," he said thoughtfully. "Toby and I have been talking about doing a song together."

"Well, that riff right there is a grand start," said Owen. "You just need to follow on and see where the rest of the song goes." There was a pause. "What's the matter? You were looking a bit round the bend there."

You just need to follow on and see where the rest of the song goes.

Josh shook his head. "I'm just surprised at how attuned we are."

Owen smiled. "I hope I can be in on it when you two lads crank it out," he said.

"No way we'd leave you out. We need a seasoned percussionist's expertise."

. . .

As soon as he had some time, Josh found Toby and played his new melody line for him. When it ended, the bassist sat with closed eyes for a few moments. Then, "Sweet!" he said. "Right there in those opening bars is the backbone of our song."

The pair set about to work out an addition to the melody

line, but nothing suited them. They labored for hours, trying various follow-ons to the beginning, but in all the notes and chords they tried, their sensitive natures couldn't find what they were looking for.

Toby said, "It's like a path you've followed that leads to the edge of a cliff, and you can't find a way across the chasm."

Josh nodded. Then he sighed and said, "Let's let it breathe. We'll both have that hook playing in our heads and maybe something will come to us."

In the days that followed, rehearsals with the band kept their minds so occupied and absorbed that they hardly had time to think. Day after day the band spent long hours in the studio, arranging and rehearsing three new tunes that Bill and Jimmy had cranked out. The room was crowded, the band having added three female backup singers, two trumpet players, and a trombone man. And there were the corporate observers, writing and comparing notes in whispers, stepping out to make calls on their cell phones. The band members were uneasy with all the scrutiny.

The work on the three new songs was nerve-racking. Bill Joist would frequently stop the band in the middle of a piece to make changes and adjustments. Once when Bill's comment, "Okay, let's pick it up again," was beginning to wear on him, Josh was made to recall the early days with his own band when his JLB bandmates had resisted his own efforts at perfection.

Bill and Jimmy complained about memos they were receiving almost daily from Tiny G's minions, directing what each of the tracks should bring out. When Josh would hear the two songwriters cursing and storming about, he knew it was about the pressure they were under to keep the new music in line with the overly engineered and heavily manicured music that was currently hot.

Setbacks are just learning experiences.

—*Joy Brooke*

CHAPTER 7

UP AGAINST IT

JOSH HAD NEVER BEEN TEMPTED to use drugs, but being around this group of musicians, he had no choice but to tolerate them. He knew they were often lonely and lost. He knew about their belief that being high enabled them to play better—he also knew it was a faulty belief. And being the rookie of the band made him hesitant to be judgmental of his very talented bandmates.

Josh had begun spending more time with Bill Joist. The singer's humor was a welcome respite from the grueling rehearsal work. He wondered, since Jimmy had told him Bill was "always high," to what extent his friend's predilection for jokes depended on drugs. He was surprised when Toby took him in hand one day to warn him. "I hesitate to say this, Shu," the bass player said, "but I notice you're hanging with Joist a lot lately."

"Yeah, so?" Josh replied, a bit defensively.

"Bill is an accident waiting to happen," Toby said.

Josh frowned. "I think I can take care of myself," he muttered.

"Cool," Toby said with a smile, and walked away.

. . .

One evening Josh and Bill were having a late dinner in a diner Bill had driven to outside of town, away from the hotel. "I get so tired of fancy restaurant food," said Bill, downing a handful of french fries. "This kind of here's-the-food place is more my style." Josh smiled, enjoying his hamburger. He had been noticing Bill's eyes straying behind him to a far corner of the dining room. *A woman, no doubt*, Josh told himself.

When they finished dinner and paid, Bill led the way out to the darkened parking lot. As they trudged to the car, Josh wondered why his friend had parked so far from the restaurant. His questions were answered when he saw a dark shape by the car and heard Bill say, "That you, Denny?" The man murmured his assent and Bill told Josh, "I'll just be a minute." He and the stranger walked over to a chain-link fence at the edge of the lot and Josh saw Bill take his wallet from his jeans.

Suddenly a blinding light was focused on the pair and a voice said loudly, "Cincinnati PD. Hands in the air!" Joist and his friend, blinded by the searchlight, turned and raised their hands. Two uniformed officers approached them and took things out of their hands. After a moment of examination of those items, the two were handcuffed and led toward a squad car. Josh heard Bill Joist's loud voice irreverently chanting the theme from *Jaws*: "Duh-duh-*duh*-duh, Duh-duh-*duh*-duh." Josh had stood rooted to the spot, feeling his heart slugging. Now a voice spoke from behind him, "You too, druggie!" He felt his arms grabbed, his wrists pinned together, and cold steel snapped around them.

. . .

The waiting, the routine booking, the sordidness of it all, was a blur behind him. Now as he sat in the jail cell with five other men, Josh knew despair. Bill had assured him, "Hey, ain't nothin' to this." But the cramped quarters, the smell of his cellmates, the constant noise throughout the jail—shouts and mumblings of drunks, heavy doors banging, complaints from those who wanted to sleep—made Josh feel lost and forgotten. Sitting there on the hard cell bench, filled with fear, confusion, and sadness, he asked himself again and again, *How in the world did I get here?* He remembered the phone call he had been allowed to make after he was booked.

"Hi, honey. I'm in jail."

"Right. Don't joke about that." Silence. "You're *serious!*"

"Yes. I was with Joist when he tried to buy drugs. The cops were waiting. I don't know if the supplier was in on it or not. But we're in jail, and I'm being treated like I was in on the deal, too."

"Oh, honey!" Joy's tone of shock was edged with contempt. He stood there in the busy hallway of the police station, feeling all eyes on him, and he was ashamed. He was sharing the details of the bust when he felt a tap on his shoulder.

A policewoman said, "Time's up."

"So, I gotta go. I'm so sorry, honey. I'll let you know what happens. I love you. Bye."

When the hullabaloo of the jail quieted down that night, Josh lay awake. He was thinking about how these men were not so different from himself. They were lying awake like he was, alone and remembering the broken pattern of their lives: chances gone, ambitions unfulfilled, the faces of women shining out of the past. He knew in these men, as in himself and his bandmates, the sense of some great adventure passing them by. What, in the end, was it all about? Everyone was after something they rarely got. And when they got it, they still weren't satisfied. There was something else to it all, something real that people, in all their rushing around to get what they wanted, failed to recognize until it was too late. *I don't want to get to the end and realize it was all for nothing. I don't want to die with my best songs still locked inside me!* He yawned and turned over. Grampa would know what it was. He fell asleep.

I don't want to get to the end and realize it was all for nothing. I don't want to die with my best songs locked inside me!

Four days. The boredom was palpable. Josh hadn't slept much and the waiting was wearing him thin and nervous. Bill's presence wasn't much comfort; the man kept making jokes, but they weren't funny. Josh looked at his friend, unshaven and bleary-eyed, showing more and more the effects of doing without his daily round of self-medication. Thinking about Grampa's words again, Josh felt regret. On the fifth day, looking tired and distraught, Bill told Josh, "The band has a date coming up this weekend. They've got to call us before a judge before then!"

Later that day, they were released. When they returned to the hotel and asked about it, Jimmy Keno said, "Tiny G fixed it up." Josh showered and shaved and went to the hotel dining room for dinner. Lingering over his meal, he wondered what Tiny G thought of him. More importantly, he wondered what Joy thought, and what the children would one day think, now that their father had a record. Finally, he wondered what Grampa would think. *I should call him.* This time the thought resulted in action.

He dialed the number. As he listened to the phone ringing on the other end, he thought, *I was stupid to avoid talking to Grampa that last time. I'm going to tell him everything.* When the phone was answered, he was surprised to hear his mother's voice on the line. "Mom? It's Josh. How are you?"

"Oh, Josh, we're not doing so well here. Grampa had a massive stroke yesterday and . . . well . . . the doctors say he may only have a few days to live."

"A stroke? Grampa? How? He's so healthy!" Shocked by the news, Josh was saying whatever came into his head.

"I know, dear. But this isn't the first of these he's had. You and your grampa have been out of touch for a while."

"Mom, I've gotta come home!"

"Yes, I think that's best. Grampa's been asking for you."

"I'll get a flight today."

"You'd better hurry."

. . .

In the plane, his mother's words kept coming back: *You and your grampa have been out of touch for a while.* He felt guilt at his lack of visits or phone calls to the old man. But there was something deeper, something that had been resounding throughout the years since he'd signed on with Tawna and started to play in the big time. It wasn't just guilt or shame; it was an agonizing grief that reached down into him and brought his whole life into focus. *It's my heart*, he finally told himself. *It's my heart that's been out of touch with his heart.* Once brought to light, this discovery claimed him. He went over and over it in his mind. It was as if he were waking up. He willed the plane to go faster.

. . .

When Josh entered the hospital room, he found it crowded with Grampa's family and friends. Josh's mother and sister came to him, hugged him, and led him to the old man's bedside. Josh was shocked to see the once robust and healthy man shriveled to this form under the covers. He felt a helpless rage, knowing that he could do nothing about the deterioration. "Hi, Grampa," he managed.

The old man opened his eyes. The ghost of a smile played across his lips. "You, boy," he said. Deep pleasure at seeing Josh shone in his eyes and sounded in his voice.

"Grampa," Josh said through his tears, "I'm sorry it's been so long . . ."

"No, no words like that, boy. I am just so happy to see you."

"How are you doing?" Josh said, sitting down on the chair next to the hospital bed.

"Aw, body's not so good," the low voice came. For a moment, the old fire flared in the now-dimmed eyes. "Inside I'm, what they say, spry as ever." He reached out, took his grandson's hand in his own bony ones, and smiled. "Josh, I love so much your coming back to me *now* . . ." He paused, and Josh caught Grampa's emphasis on the time. "I always saw what you are, such a *brafied*. Your music, yeah, it's so good, but more than that, I know you can let your pure self come through. That's the song you really are. I hear you are doing great, boy. 'Specially like it that you're writing songs."

The ailing elder paused, as if to catch his breath. He then motioned to Josh's mother, who brought a small wooden item to the bed. In his weakened state, Grampa fingered the piece lightly, then passed it feebly down to Josh. "Last thing I finished before being placed here. Far from my best work, but still hope it'll speak to you, son." Upon hearing Grampa call him "son," Josh's heart seized, reflecting a mixture of great warmth paired with intense grief. This man was the only father figure Josh had ever really known. Josh peered into his hands, which now held a plaque. His name was written on it. The simple letters were somewhat bent and a little uneven in height, but the plaque's message could not have been more straightforward. It read:

> *Be Strong and Courageous.*
> —JOSHUA 1:9

After passing down the carved gift to Josh, Grampa coughed painfully for a while. "Fix my pillows. Grampa's got some things to tell you."

Josh noted the earnest look in his grandfather's red-rimmed gray eyes. "Okay, Grampa."

"Okay. You are in, what you call, a big band, eh?" Josh nodded. "Very exciting. Very exciting. You are really in 'the business' now, eh? Eh?" the man repeated.

"Yes, Grampa." Josh said, wondering what this was leading to.

The emaciated figure in the hospital bed was long silent. "So, I tell you of a fish—" He was suddenly racked by another coughing spell. The others held his arms to support him. When the attack died, he looked at Josh, eyes suddenly lit with the old fire. "You hear? A fish!"

"A fish, Grampa?" Josh said, wondering if the old man's mind was weakened.

"Aye. Someone told the fish he was in water. The fish looked around and said, 'Water? What water?'"

"Ah," Josh said. "The fish was so used to the water, he didn't see it."

Grampa nodded. "This is like that."

The coughing came again, more painful this time. It took the old man a while to catch his breath afterward. Then he said, "I think when you . . . play with the famous ones, you want to be like them, eh?"

"Sure," Josh said with enthusiasm.

"But that's the danger, Josh," Grampa said. "You're the fish, and all around you is the water—everyone trying to be like everyone else but not knowing how it robs them. When you try to be like others, you don't listen to yourself. You can't hear your own voice. You can't find your own song!"

When you try to be like others, you don't listen to yourself. You can't hear your own voice. You can't find your own song!

Grampa had risen off his pillows, but with these last words a rasping came from his throat. He sank down and closed his eyes. Someone went for the nurse, who came and bent over the old man, touching his neck. She did some other checking and finally turned to Josh and his mother and shook her head. "I'm so sorry," she said. "He's gone."

Josh felt a stab inside, tears dimming his eyes. In a few seconds, he had seen the life force depart in someone he had treasured all his years. He remembered the passion with which the old man's last words were spoken, and he knew his grandfather had put all his remaining strength into them. Those words were indelibly etched in Josh's consciousness now. Then the single Welsh word his grampa had used to describe him came back to him. *I remember it from growing up. People said* brafied *to mean something really fine and incredibly special. And that's what he called me.*

After Grampa's funeral, Josh returned to Cincinnati and took up his duties with the band. And yet, he was different inside. His loss had left him chastened and humbled, determined to somehow honor the old man through his efforts. *Grampa's final handiwork was to create a sign for me, incorporating a phrase that called me by name,* Josh marveled. And then, each time his mind returned to those last words of warning Grampa had spoken, Josh would feel a quiet sense of wonder. *The last thing that great man said, in his entire life— eighty-some years—was for me. Just for me! Did Grampa stay alive as long as he did just to give me that plaque and the blessing, or the warning—or both?*

For the next four months, the group worked on their new album. Whenever they could find time to work on their song—which was often at night—the three comrades hastened to the practice room, where Josh and Toby plugged in their guitars and Owen seated himself at the drum kit. Then they went to work on their unfinished song. They worked long and hard and gradually parts of the song came into focus, but the ending still eluded them. One evening when they took a break, they talked about the band.

"I think we're watching Tawna's slide into mediocrity," Toby said.

"It's really sad," said Josh. "I don't like the lyrics that corporate's got Bill and Jimmy writing. If they're not cheesy, they're trashy. All Tiny G thinks about is being up to date with the squalid stuff that's out there."

"Yeah," Owen put in. "It's all about the bleedin' money."

The conversation among the three gifted musicians was reflective of a larger trend in the music business. Like other forms of entertainment such as movies and television, music had begun to explore what some commentators called the dark underbelly of society. It was as if the lowest elements of human experience were being scrutinized and exposed for the herd. The success of the corporate machine was based on a simple truth: if popular tastes were fed long enough on this fare, they would soon demand it. As Josh, Toby, and Owen watched Tawna become infected with this virus, they felt it as an insult to their very souls.

. . .

During these days, whenever Josh, Owen, or Toby came upon one another, they would exchange a nod or know-ing look. They were acknowledging that although their days were filled with the discouraging work on the album's lurid tracks, there was something finer bubbling on a back burner, something that promised genuine gratification of their tastes and talents.

. . .

When Josh retired at 2:00 a.m. after one of their private practices, he lay in bed thinking. As he was drifting to sleep a memory came to him. When he was a young boy, Grampa had often taken him on walks deep in the woods, teach-ing him to identify the sounds of birds, squirrels, and other creatures. The lessons were in what the old man called "deep listening." Grampa showed him how to walk silently, placing each step slowly and carefully. Once, the elder brought him to a stop and said, "Shh. You hear that?" Josh listened but could hear nothing but the call of a crow far overhead. "Mister Snake was getting out of our way," Grampa said. Bending down, he pointed to a track in the mud. "See? He was here."

As Josh lay contemplating that memory, he realized, *All this chasing after the music is a waste of energy. I have to be quiet and listen, the way Grampa taught me back there in the woods. If I do that, I'll hear it when it shows up.*

. . .

One night the trio met in the studio and prepared to work as usual. They played the unfinished song and, when they reached the point where they'd run out of ideas, Owen and Toby stopped; but Josh played on as if he knew the way. It was a new connection that signified completion. Owen and Toby waited expectantly while Josh added new notations to the lead sheet. Toby looked at them and without a pause added the final words of the song under the score. Then the team played the song all the way through for the first time. They stared at one another in awe: *Did we really do this? Is it really finished?*

The song, "Born Knowing," began by expressing quiet confidence in a love apparently destined from the ages. Then halfway through, the joyous melody changed to a lament: the relationship had proved ill-fated. For the singer who had been "born knowing," the lifelong dream was wiped away. The reappearance of Josh's powerful guitar hook wove the story together, and the turning point in Toby's lyrics was crafted to produce a subtle wrench in the listener's emotions.

"If this ain't a hit," Owen said, shaking his head. The others nodded, still in wonder.

And they were right. They chose a time just before their lunch break the next day, after a morning of grinding rehearsal, for their announcement. Toby was the spokesman. "Some of you know that Josh and I, along with Owen, have been working on a song after hours. We finished it yesterday, and we want to play it for you."

The trio played "Born Knowing," with Josh singing. The moment their performance was finished, there were cheers of delight and expressions of admiration. "How did you guys come up with that?" and "It's genius!" and "Wait'll Tiny hears this one!" Bill Joist said, "I think I'm gonna cry." When the others looked at him, he said, "Hey, I mean it. For once, I'm not making a bad joke!"

Josh and his friends were gratified that their bandmates immediately recognized the mastery behind the song. And the company welcomed it as the jewel in the collection. In fact, "Born Knowing" became the album's title.

The new song seemed to buoy the band's expectations and it wasn't long before Keno and Joist drew on their original talents to come up with a choice addition, an uplifting track with the title of "Generosity."

The album release came just before the holidays and, with the start of a new year, the band was on the road again, performing the new songs. Many fans liked the pieces the bandmates called the "noisy ones," but the highest sales of singles from the album were first for "Born Knowing" and then "Generosity."

Josh liked watching the crowds mouthing the words when Tawna played his song, but after a second year of nonstop touring with shouting crowds, endless nights, and sterile hotel rooms, the road was taking its toll on him. His hope for a good night's sleep and a decent diet was a distant memory. He was visibly thinner. He wore makeup on stage to cover the dark rings under his eyes. Some mornings after shaving he would look in the mirror and think, *I'm starting to look like one of those scrawny, wasted rock guys. Am I becoming one of them?*

Often it takes some calamity to make us live in the present. Then suddenly we wake up and see all the mistakes we have made.

—*Bill Watterson*

CHAPTER 8

MISFORTUNE'S BLOWS

AT THE BEGINNING OF HIS YEARS on the road, Josh had made it a point to be home for a few days at least every two weeks. Each summer he, Joy, and the girls would spend several weeks at Grampa's lakeside cottage. This was a time for building precious memories as a family, and for Beth and Sarah Grace to get to know their great-grandfather. The old man's love for them was deep and constant.

As the years passed, Josh's home visits became less frequent. Soon they were more or less monthly. From the time Beth was born with cystic fibrosis, it had been understood that Joy would be Beth's primary caregiver. As Josh's absences lengthened, he had little time to participate in all that it took to protect Beth from the lung diseases that accounted for so many early deaths in young people. While away from home, he relied on reports from Joy, and later on conversations with Beth, to keep track of her progress.

These were important growing-up years for his daughters, and it pained Josh to have so little time with them. The memory of his own father's absence haunted him, and he tried to make each time home "special," frequently taking the family out to eat, to movies, to amusement parks, etc. Joy once told him, "Your job isn't to be the entertainment director for your kids, but their father and friend." Early on, she coached Josh to develop the habit of writing letters to his kids while he was away. Though he always spoke to each of them when he called from the road, his letters were precious to the girls. And then the letters, too, became more infrequent.

One day, Josh received a letter from Joy and, as he opened it, he felt a pang of fear. The letter read:

Dearest Josh,

As you know, our children are growing up without a father. In many ways their situation is similar to your own, although you never really had a dad in your life to begin with. And yet in the most important way—not being around to watch and listen to them and to be with them as they experience all the wonders and pains of growing up—it is the same.

We certainly did not plan for things to turn out this way. Before the children came, our marriage worked wonderfully. But as your absences grow longer, that is changing. They say that absence makes the heart grow fonder but, in this case, it doesn't seem to work that way. Sometimes I have to look at your picture to remember what you look like, but I can't love a picture.

*For the girls and for me, there's just a big father/
husband hole that needs filling. Your infrequent visits
home—"visit" is a good word, as you are more like a
visitor—do not serve to fill it. Each one begins with
gladness, but ends in fresh sadness, for your going away
again leaves that hole.*

*I did not figure on a long-distance marriage. It
leaves unfulfilled the part of me that needs to give and
receive affection with a mate. I have kept up my part
of the bargain as a parent, and it has not been easy. I
haven't told you of the countless times Mom and I wondered if Beth would make it. To say nothing of our Sweet
Sarah Grace, who barely knows you.*

*Josh, you have provided us a good living, but I am
sad to say you have not kept the agreement that was
implicit in your vows to me, to provide a good life. I
don't know what to do about that, but whatever is to be
done will be done soon.*

With love and tears,
 Joy

Upon reading Joy's letter, Josh's mind became a jumble of
dark thoughts. It was easy for him to use disappointment to
prove himself a failure. *What has my life become? I knew this
would happen! Things never turn out! I knew I was no good.* He
went about the next hours in a complete funk. In the end,
however, his depression did not prevent him from taking
action. Despite his despair, he knew he had to do something. He was on a plane to Seattle that very evening.

When he arrived home, he used his key to let himself
in and climbed the stairs to Joy's bedroom. Hearing him

enter, she'd sat up in bed. He sat down and embraced her tearfully, holding her a long time. Her body was warm from sleep, but it felt frail and small to his arms—and unresponsive. "Honey," he said, "I couldn't wait to get here after reading your letter. You were absolutely right in everything you said. I want our marriage more than anything." He sat back, looking into her eyes. "I will do anything it takes, including quitting Tawna . . ."

It was easy for him to use disappointment to prove himself a failure . . . Despite his despair, he knew he had to do something.

Joy's voice was quiet and factual in tone. "You can't quit the band, Josh. You still have two years on your contract."

"I know, but I don't care. I'll get out of it. I don't want to keep up with this crazy lifestyle anyway. I want to be a husband and dad, like I should be."

Joy sat with her eyes resting downward. She was silent a long time. "Josh," she finally said, "please sit over there." Obediently he left the bed and sat in a chair.

When she looked at him, in her eyes were both hurt and deep resolve. Her voice was careful, measured. "This is not easy to say, but I'm going to say it. Things have been this way too long. It's going to take a lot to win me back."

"I get you," he said, trying to sound calm. But her words had paralyzed him. In a moment, the old unworthiness engulfed him in its dark cloud. The enormity of his situation made him lose his breath. Finally, he murmured, "I don't know what to say."

A silence ensued. "I think you'd better go, then," Joy said. "When you do know what to say, you can call me."

Josh rose and made his way downstairs. Passing the girls' rooms, he choked back a sob. He stumbled from the house, got into his rented car, and drove slowly away. He found a motel and rang the office doorbell until the owner awakened and was kind enough to open and register him. The night was sleepless. He lay like a stone, frozen with grief. How could he have let this go on for so long? Why hadn't he seen the signs?

When morning came, he went to the motel office. The proprietor told him in a cheery voice, "You save ten percent if you stay three nights." On impulse, Josh shrugged and agreed. He spent the day driving around, wondering how a place he called his hometown could look so alien. The vision of Joy's face, the look he had last seen in her eyes, haunted him.

That evening, he thought to check his email. There were messages from Toby and Tiny G. He called Toby's number. "Shu, where'd you go, dude?" his friend said. "People been asking about you." Josh explained as best he could. Toby listened, then said soberly, "Well, your running off may not have gone over with Tiny. His scouts let him know right away that you cut out and that you missed practice today."

"Yeah, well, too bad," Josh said. "I've got a situation here I can't walk away from. I've done way too much of that already."

"I hear you, man. I still think you better call Tiny."

It was eight o'clock. Josh went to a restaurant for his

first meal of the day. He sat over his food, thinking about the call and avoiding it. His words to Toby had been mere bravado. *I'm never any good dealing with Tiny*, he thought. *What's he going to say?* Back in his car, he drove out of town and continued slowly down a country road. Finally pulling over to the side of the road, he turned off the engine and dialed Tiny's number.

"Hello, Josh." Hearing that oily voice, Josh visualized the enormous bulk of the speaker. "I've been waiting to hear from you."

"I know. I'm sorry to—"

"Have you read your contract lately, Josh?" Tiny G said.

"Well, no, I—"

"It doesn't allow you to just pick up and leave when you feel like it. You are obligated, Josh. Obligated."

"I know."

"Actually, my friend," the fat man said in a lighter tone, "you may have done me a favor."

"How . . . how's that?"

"I've been grooming an excellent guitar man for some months who I think would make a fine lead for Tawna."

Josh paused to swallow. "But I'm the lead guitarist for Tawna."

"You were, my friend, you were. As of now, my lawyers have prepared the documents for your termination. These will be mailed to you, along with your, shall we say, effects from here. The guitar you've been using will, of course, not be among them. Have you any questions?"

"Yes, I do. What about my family? I'm their sole

provider—their only source of support. Please. You can't do this to me."

A long pause. Then: "I think we are done here."

Josh would dwell many times over the next three years on the results of his choice to devote his energies to his career and to neglect his family. His old friendship with Danny was his occasional conduit to news of his loved ones. He kept up with reports, learning that Joy sold the home they had purchased during his early years on the road. Soon Joy secured a good nursing job at a nearby clinic and moved herself and the girls to a suitable apartment near her work, which also accommodated her mother, Susanna. Beth and Sarah Grace remained in the same school district with their friends, and Susanna was there to greet them when they returned from school. Between the funds from the sale of the house, the money saved from Josh's high-earning years with Tawna, and Joy's salary, the little family was able to live well.

Simone Weil has written, "Two prisoners whose cells adjoin communicate with each other by knocking on the wall. The wall is the thing which separates them but is also their means of communication. It is the same with us and God. Every separation is a link." Although the love that Josh and Joy shared could not be communicated in words over the months and years of their separation, each felt it deeply and painfully.

Muddy water, let stand, becomes clear.

—Lao Tzu

CHAPTER 9

HEAD FOR AP JACK!

DEEP FOREST FASTNESSES, EVERGREENS and maples with occasional stands of birch, swept by on either side of the road. Ahead, the familiar foothills reared their heads. Joshua knew the way well. All his life he'd made this trip, first with his grandfather, mother, and sister, and later with his wife and daughters. Never had he come alone. Throughout the drive, his thoughts went back to his grampa.

As Joshua reached the top of a hill and rounded a bend, the dark shape of Ap Jack stood out against the moonlit sky. The spectacle of the mountain, with the lake beneath it bathed in a pathway of moonshine, uplifted his long-downtrodden spirits. As he began the descent to the lakefront, he felt a great relief flooding his heart.

It was as if the spirit that was Grampa had pulled him

here—away from his sad, meaningless life as a paid-by-the-hour music teacher—by the unconquerable force of love. Joshua's coming had been spur of the moment, on the heels of his dream about the freak summer storm, and the soulless day that had ensued. But now that he was here, it was clear to him how much he needed time away. Looking up at the beloved peak, he whispered, *Grampa, I know it's you who have led me here. Thank you for the blessing of your company that I feel right now.*

He drove through the tiny village of Tenby, dark and asleep, and turned along the shore road that led to Grampa's cabin. Stepping up on the porch, he looked up at the sign over the front door, carved by Grampa: *Mawr Glas Heron.* Grampa had loved the great blue herons that nested and fished in the reeds across the lake, where he and Josh had often paddled to watch them. He had given his cottage the Welsh name for the graceful bird.

Entering the old place, Joshua savored its rich odors of wood and resin, even the musty smell of a place shut up for many months. It had been several summers since he and Joy and the girls had spent time here and, standing in the little kitchen, he regretted that sorely.

Everywhere were signs of Grampa's years here—carved loons, paintings of the mountain, photos of the old man and his family. As Joshua looked at his own image in those pictures and relived those times, a lump rose in his throat. He looked up into the cockpits of the kayaks that he and Grampa had used so many times, stored upside-down on the beams overhead. He resolved to take one down and go paddling the next day.

. . .

After a few days at the lake, Joshua began to set the cabin and its sheds in order, doing a few minor chores each day. Grampa's extensive collection of carpentry and instrument-making tools were of great value to him. Just holding them in his hands moved him to remember the man who had been his lifelong mentor and example. Often in appreciation, he would repeat the phrase *A life well lived*.

One morning he followed a steep wooded trail that wound partway up Ap Jack. With each of its rocky turns, memories came back of ascending this path with Grampa. Always, as they climbed, the old man would share his memories of finding the trail as a boy. But his words would die away to a reverent silence as they neared their destination. For at the end of the trail stood The Tree.

A massive bur oak over eighty feet tall, it was a mighty sight to behold. The coarsely textured crown, wild and woolly acorns, and massive trunk with rough and deeply furrowed bark never failed to arouse awe in both man and boy. Seating himself now at its crumpled feet, he gazed out at the breathless expanse of valley.

Once, he had caught sight of a young bald eagle, high against the blue. Grampa had told him the mighty bird can live up to fifty years. They had looked for the nest, but never found it. Now this bird was tracing the same lazy circles in the sky that its parent had. As Joshua sat alone at the foot of the patriarch oak, watching cloud shadows move across the valley and missing his beloved old woodsman, occasional brown leaves sifted down and reminded him that fall was coming.

Since being at the lake, Joshua's mind would go back to one winter when he and his best friend, Danny, had spent a week there as teens, snowshoeing and ice fishing. One day, on impulse, he pulled out his cell phone and dialed a number on its list, wondering if it was current. The voice that answered left no doubt, and it lifted Joshua's heart to hear his childhood name invoked with such anticipation.

"Josh!"

"Hi, Dan."

"Where are you?"

"I'm at the lake. I thought you might—"

"I'm on my way!"

From the moment Danny arrived, the two old companions felt not a particle of distance. They hugged heartily and brushed away tears, enjoying the feeling of picking up where they had left off. As Danny was unloading his car, Josh said, "Did you bring your drums?" Danny pulled a long case from the backseat, saying, "No drums, but this keyboard's got all the drum sounds."

Josh had long known that Danny had married his sweetheart Marcia Donnegan, who had been Joy's best friend in high school. As they walked the village main street to Davies' tiny food market, he begged for details.

"Marcia and I have two boys, Will and Ted," Danny told him. "Marcia sends her love. She knows what this time means to us, and she told me to stay as long as I can. She works at the library, and I work as a trainer for an operations management software company. I can take some time off because I've racked up a lot of extra vacation days. I also play weddings, bar mitzvahs, and occasional gigs around town. I don't have any gigs planned for weeks."

"Still got those great chops?"

"I guess, but you're the band boy. I told you years back that I was going to be your greatest fan. I've kept track of all your moves."

"Yeah," Josh said, "including the latest."

"Hey, it happens. That's the music business for you."

Josh offered up an insight he hadn't expected to share, nor did he fully understand the words as they expressed themselves. "Out on the road with Tawna, I had it all, living what most would call an absolute dream. My life was surrounded by tens of thousands of adoring fans and I was rarely, if ever, truly alone. And yet, I had never been lonelier in all my life. Sure, I had lots of cool toys, but no one truly special to share them with. I had never made so much money before . . . nor been so miserable inside.

"Nothing in this world—not fame, nor fortune, nor power, nor possessions—could replace the hole in my heart that could only be filled by my Joy. I was missing her deeply, in both my mind and my soul. I didn't even realize it at the time, but I would have gladly given it all away just to have Joy back in my life."

Nothing can ever replace the joy that calls out to our spirit, and the community of our closest family and truest friends. These are the pearls of greatest price.

Danny absorbed Josh's deep pronouncement, letting the heaviness in Josh's words diffuse in their momentary silence. He then countered with a simple acknowledgment: "Well, I've heard nothing can ever replace the joy that calls out to our spirit, and the community of our closest family and truest friends. These are the pearls of greatest value."

Josh nodded his head in solemn recognition, then lightened up when he realized Danny's comment made him think about their other former Josh Lynk Band members. "Hey, what's up with our old JLB bandmates these days?" Josh asked.

"Both married with kids," Danny said. "Greg stayed on with his dad's insurance business and he has pretty much taken it over. He says he's having a great time supporting people's livelihoods with his products. It's like a business version of how he supported us in the band. You know, Greg was never comfortable taking a lot of risk, so insurance sounds perfect for him!" Danny laughed.

"That's so cool," Josh replied. "I remember one of the last conversations I had with my dad. He said he thought I might be a swim teacher one day, or maybe own a bar, or work in one with him. I guess—I can only guess—he did have his own sort of dreams or expectations of me . . . apparently involving liquid!" Josh couldn't help but to crack up at the central theme he found in an otherwise somber comment.

"Anyway, what about Colin?" Josh inquired.

"Remember how Colin always liked the limelight? He was such a natural at dealing with different kinds of people. He found his niche as a sales guy, when he went to work for Hamlin selling pianos and keyboards. I think he found out about the company from a Hamlin board member he happened to meet in Dallas, after one of our concerts. Funny how things work out, sometimes."

Reveling in the warmth of their renewed friendship, Joshua and Danny continued to reminisce about their adventures together.

One afternoon, they entered the cabin after a swim, laughing at the puddles they left on the old lined wooden floor. Joshua had already used the few towels he had found, and the two began searching for more. "Found some," Danny said, pointing to the top shelf of the bedroom closet.

When Josh removed the pile of linens, he saw a cardboard shoe box at the back. He lifted it down, wondering at its contents, and placed it on the bed. When he opened it, both men caught their breath. The box was filled with poems and music sheets, written out in Grampa's careful hand. They stared at each other. Taking the box into the main room, Josh placed it on the teak-root coffee table. "Did you ever know Grampa was a songwriter?" Danny said.

Josh shook his head. "No, but he was everything else related to music. Why not a lyricist?"

"So, he must've kept these notes a secret."

Josh nodded and, after a silence, his and Danny's eyes sparkled. "Maybe so we'd find them!" they chorused.

Joshua was remembering the old man's teachings about how a strong intention worked, continuing to produce results in the world that were not clear at the time. "I can just feel him looking in on us here," he said with eyes glistening. "And smiling!"

"Maybe you want to look at these alone," Danny said.

"Are you kidding? When Grampa meant for both of us to find them?" Josh lifted out the first sheet. It contained relatively plain and simple words, with no associated musical score. "Should I read it?" he asked. At Danny's nod, he read aloud:

What do you see when you look in a mirror?

It's a disguise

Just a disguise

But if you are wise you'll know who is looking

Through your eyes

Through your eyes

You are in truth a child of grace

From beyond a distant star

Try to discern behind that face

The made-for-amazing one you are.

You are a song to be sung to the world

Believe it's true

When light shines through

You'll help others believe they're made for

Amazing, too

Amazing, too.

"Wow," Danny said. "Read it again, will you?" Joshua read the poem aloud a second time. He knew that Danny, himself a gifted songwriter, was concentrating not only on the message, but the rhyme scheme, which seemed very old-style to him. "What do you think?" he asked.

"It's a powerful message," Danny said, "a universal one. It makes the listener ponder." He added, "It makes *me* ponder!"

"And?" Joshua said, fishing for more.

"Well," Danny said, frowning, "I'm thinking how your grampa grew up singing and playing all the old show tunes, the standards. That was a different era."

"True." Joshua noted that Danny was looking uncomfortable. "So?"

"So, what if you and I came up with an updated musical arrangement of this, the way we used to?"

Joshua beamed. "I was thinking the same thing. Make the lyrics more for today's audience, and use a modern melody."

"Exactly." Danny frowned. "You don't think that's, like, desecrating it?"

"No way!"

Later Josh saw Danny studying one of the signs, hand-carved in various woods, that Grampa had posted around the cabin. "Did you ever read this?" he said. The sign read:

> *He will take great delight in you,*
> *he will quiet you with his love,*
> *He will rejoice over you with singing.*
> —ZEPHANIAH 3:17

Danny said, "I knew your grampa was a musician, and he made and restored instruments, but ever since reading that lyric of his and noticing these reminders he put up all around the place, I see he must have been a deeply spiritual man."

"He was." Josh felt sorry he had not imparted this important aspect of his grandfather's nature to Danny. "In fact," he added, "Grampa has been my spiritual coach ever since I was small. Not that I have been much of a student. Many times, I would listen to Grampa, but I'm not sure how much I actually heard."

Danny headed off Josh's subtle negative volley before it could build up additional steam and derail him. "Well, it seems like his messages got through to you more than you realized. I mean, there's no question as to the positive influence your grampa has had on your life. It sounds like he's still coaching you."

"That's for sure," Josh said, abruptly righting his tone and tenor.

Danny said, "Here's another one I like." He led Josh to a verse that hung between the front windows. It read:

> *Before they call, I will answer.*
> *While they are yet speaking, I will hear.*
> —ISAIAH 65:24

Danny said, "Sounds like a divine serendipity—the answer's on the way, even before we think to ask for it."

Josh nodded. "I think Grampa would add, 'First make sure you're tuned in.' He used to tell me to think of myself as an instrument that needed to stay in tune."

"That's a good way for us to go."

"You mean in collaborating to make music inspired by him?"

"Exactly."

Josh smiled. "If one of these songs ever makes it, we should have you, me, and Bryn Lynk listed as cowriters."

Knowing yourself is
the beginning of all wisdom.

—Aristotle

CHAPTER 10

A SEARCH

IN THE DAYS THAT FOLLOWED, Joshua's mind continued to entertain memory flashes of Grampa. Living in the old man's house was bringing back many of his teachings across the years. With Danny's prompting, he began to study more of the small hand-carved aphorisms that adorned the cabin with wisdom. The irony of one particular quote puzzled him. It read: *Your visions will become clear only when you can look into your own heart. Who looks outside, dreams; who looks inside, awakes.* What, he wondered, did Carl Jung mean by the phrase, "who looks inside, awakes"? Josh was beginning to realize that in the hurry and rush to get ahead in his life as a musician, he might have neglected something important. But what was it?

What, for instance, had Grampa meant that time he gave Josh a beautiful hand-carved ukulele for his birthday and said, "It's because of what's within ya, lad." When Josh had asked, "What do you mean 'within me,' Grampa?" the old man had changed the subject. Now the question rang with more insistence.

Your visions will become clear only when you can look into your own heart. Who looks outside, dreams; who looks inside, awakes.
—Carl Jung

Grampa had carved another quote, this one from Elizabeth Gilbert, into a wooden sign: *Your treasure—your perfection—is within you already. But to claim it, you must leave the busy commotion of the mind and . . . enter into the silence of the heart.* Josh pondered the words. He knew no one can be perfect, yet he couldn't help wondering why Grampa would take hours to carve it into a sign. *I feel like it's a direct conduit from Grampa to me.*

Josh wondered how to do what the author was expressing. *I've heard people talk about meditation. Stuff like that has never interested me. Maybe I just haven't understood it.*

. . .

His visiting and working with Danny had been taking up much of each day. They went boating and swimming and scouted the wooded trails, but Josh found himself more and more wanting to get away and hike alone. Finally, he said, "What do you say we plan to spend some hours apart each day?" Fearing he might offend his friend, he was relieved when Danny said, "Weird how much we think alike. I was going to suggest the same thing."

Joshua began making visits to The Tree; soon the hike became the centerpiece of each day. He carried scraps of paper on which he'd written aphorisms and notes from his thoughts about Grampa. Soon these became unmanageable, so he bought a small blank-paged journal at the bookstore. He was inspired in part by one of Grampa's self-created notebooks he had simply titled "Grace Notes." Grampa's little notebook reminded Josh of his daughter, Sarah Grace; Josh noted how "Sweet Grace"—the nickname he had given his youngest—reminded him of Grampa. Humbled and amazed at this thought, Josh was struck by the truth that grace can be a name, a feeling, and a sound—all-at-once.

Emerson, Thoreau, the Bible, and Lao Tzu became just a few of Josh's many favorites from Grampa's library; his copybook pages were filling up rapidly with their words. He began copying quotes and passages on the left-hand side and using the pages on the right to capture his own feelings and experiences. Soon this writing became an everyday entry, and an important part of Josh's day.

The more time he spent alone in nature, the more he thought about Grampa's words, the more he understood the irony in Jung's phrase "who looks inside, awakes." Though he had little interest in meditation, immersing his mind in the works of great thinkers began to send his focus "inside." Something was definitely stirring within him. He was listening more. Maybe he was doing what Grampa had called journeying, a solo musician's way of following a melody's inner path, rather than trying to compose it.

He could hardly understand his delight with one quote by Lao Tzu, which read: *A good traveler has no fixed plans, and is not intent on arriving.* Seeming in direct opposition to the way he'd lived his life, it felt comfortable now, like Grampa's life, like the way he wanted to live.

One day when he was at The Tree, he became especially calm while watching a bumblebee working some nearby blossoms. Suddenly it was as if a door opened in his mind. *Why, I've lived my whole entire life for myself! Sure, I liked providing for my family, and sure, I enjoyed entertaining crowds with my guitar playing, but at the core those were selfish things. I was proud and conceited and self-centered, even though I thought my intentions were good. While going through the motions I guess I just became full of myself. I just didn't realize how one-dimensional my motivations were. Why have I never seen this before?*

He was in wonder at the revelation. The first thought threaded into another: *How else would I live?* Which opened up further analysis: *Making others happy made me happy. In fact, my family and my fans would have had no interest in me if I hadn't been able to see that they were pleased with what I did. Maybe there's such a thing as selfish unselfishness?*

He decided to bring this up with Danny. At dinner that evening, he sought for a lead-in. "Do you think there's such a thing as being selfish by being unselfish?"

Danny put down his fork. "I've wondered about that," he said. "A lot of good has been done by folks during our lifetimes, and not only by famous people like Gandhi and Mother Teresa. For me, I know I'm happiest when I forget myself, drumming in a way that pleases my listeners. If they didn't smile and show they're enjoying it, then I honestly wouldn't be that happy. Even in my time at work, I get into a groove with people, a kind of flow that's really enjoyable. And when I see how happy my boys are when the three of us go camping, I get a real kick out of it. So, maybe there is something like—what did you call it?"

"Selfish unselfishness. Or maybe it's unselfish selfishness. Anyway, it's the pleasure you get from making others happy. I never really thought about it until I came up here as a quiet getaway and started looking back on my life. Today I was bowled over when it hit me that I've lived a very self-centered life. I don't like seeing that, but in some strange way I do because I was blind to it before. And now, talking to you, it helps me to think that—like you—I've made someone happy. If I get kicks out of that, then maybe I'm not so bad after all."

Danny looked across the table at Joshua; when he spoke, it was with unmistakable sincerity. "You've always made me happy, my friend."

"Ah, come on—"

"No. Let me explain. I've been extremely happy to have been close enough all those years watching and listening to you play guitar. It's given me a lot of satisfaction to realize what a real genius my best friend is. Why do you think I kept such good track of you when you went on? It wasn't for *your* pleasure; it was for mine. So, call it admiration or pride on my part, who cares, but you've given incredible happiness to me. And you do still. I'm having a ball being up here with you these days. Aren't you happy having me here?"

"Sure, but—"

"Okay, so having a real friend generates authentic happiness. Giving and receiving friendship can't be beat!"

The friends' deep discussion ended with laughter.

Naturally one focus for Joshua in his new habit of inner reflection was his family. That was where remorse tended to eat away at him, but with new light playing on his consciousness, his old habit of self-abasement was easing. *All my life I've thought I wasn't enough. Wonder if that, in itself, isn't a form of selfishness? They say that being all wrapped up with me, me, me leads to a big head, but the opposite way of being down on oneself is just as much of an ego thing, a self-absorption. Even though it's negative, a me-me-me habit is pretty isolating. It doesn't leave room for other people, and even makes them uncomfortable around you.*

Occasionally when his mind went on this way, he would step back and smile at himself. *What is this, anyway? Is there a shrink inside me?* But then he thought further: *No. I'm sure it's your voice I'm hearing, Grampa.*

Joshua's newfound enlightenment was something he early on wished he could share with Joy. He brought up the matter to Danny. "Do you think if I told her what I'm discovering she would just see it as—no; wait. Do you think if I told her, it would just be my way of seeking her favor?"

Instead of answering, Danny showed him a quote from the *Tao te Ching*: "He who knows does not speak. He who speaks does not know."

Autumn had begun, coloring the maples along the lake with red and yellow finery. The nights were frosty and the lake was cold for swimming, but the men continued to take their daily dips. Although no lifeguard was on duty, a few other residents braved the chill. One day Joshua heard a scream. Far out in the lake he saw a figure bobbing, arms flailing. It was a woman on the shore who had screamed. Now she was yelling frantically, "Help! That's my son! He's drowning!"

Without stopping to think, Joshua turned and plunged into the chilling water. He swam a long way, then raised up to sight the victim. When he was still fifty feet away, the head disappeared. Stroking to the spot where the boy had gone down, Josh took a huge breath and dove deep into the icy depths. As he descended, the water grew darker and more frigid. After searching an area but finding nothing, Josh felt like his lungs were about to burst. Then he made out a dimly glowing object through the murk. Reaching it and seeing it was the youngster, he grabbed an arm and kicked powerfully for the surface. As he broke through and inhaled mightily, he realized the boy's body was limp. Was he unconscious, or dead?

A man had launched a rowboat and he was there in moments. As he grasped the boy's body and lifted him into the boat, he asked Josh, "Are you all right?" Joshua replied,

"I'm fine. Just get him to shore." The man turned and rowed frantically back to the beach.

A crowd had gathered by the time Josh dragged himself weakly from the water. He was grateful when Danny supported his weight. "How's the kid?" Josh asked. "Don't know yet," Danny replied. "They're working on him." They went to where people were gathered. Someone was bent over the small body on the beach. Then Josh saw the figure move, and a cheer went up.

The boy soon recovered and sat up. When he was wrapped in a blanket and out of danger, the mother turned to the crowd. "Where's the fellow that saved my boy?" she said.

"He's over here," Danny called.

Someone in the crowd said, "Why, it's Josh Lynk." Other residents recognized Josh and came around to congratulate him. These were uncomfortable moments for the newly minted hero.

As he and Danny walked to the cabin, Danny said, "Good job, dude!"

"Ah, I didn't even think about what I was doing. It was automatic. Probably if I'd stopped to think—"

"Stuff that," Danny said. "That's the old Josh talking. How about just saying, 'thanks'?"

Joshua grinned. "Okay, then. Thanks."

. . .

The rescue episode provided new subject matter for Joshua's self-searching. He pondered the fact that he'd acted on behalf of another person without a single thought for himself. Something had compelled him into action, as if he weren't in charge of himself at all. He wondered, *Is this what writers mean when they talk about connecting with something greater than oneself?*

That evening Josh found a small sign of Grampa's making that he'd not noticed before. When he read Mother Teresa's words, *We can do no great things, only small things with great love*, he was astonished. He knew that her words could be applied to his action at the lake, but he was not clear how. He took them apart. *"We can do no great things" is what I felt there on the beach. The people acted like what I'd done was great, but I knew better. Not in the way Danny caught me up on putting myself down. I just knew in my heart it wasn't great. But then she says what we can do: "small things with great love." I know I did a small thing; was it with great love? If it was, it wasn't mine at all because I didn't feel anything—except when I saw that kid's mother so happy. Maybe love is really action, not just a feeling.*

**We can do no great things,
only small things with great love.
—Mother Teresa**

Josh continued to visit Grampa's bookshelf to mine for treasures. He told Danny, "I've always felt something I called the Grampa Connection. Up here, I'm getting used to living in a new way that I call Grampa's Way."

"What's that?"

"It means trusting and letting things take their course, then being surprised when things show up right on time.

It's happening pretty regularly through Grampa's books. For instance, I found this quote in one of his books, called *Mere Christianity*: 'Do not waste time bothering whether you love your neighbor; act as if you did.' I'd been trying to figure out my motives and feelings the other day at the lake and was getting nowhere. Finding these words made me stop wondering about this selfish-unselfish stuff, and whether I love people or don't love them. It made me want to just do what it says: act as if I do love them, and let it go at that."

Do not waste time bothering whether you love your neighbor; act as if you did.
—C.S. Lewis

"Sounds a little like 'fake it till you make it,'" Danny said.

Joshua thought about that. "I see what you mean, but I don't think it is. In the first place, you're not faking it, you're just doing it. And secondly, you don't think at all about 'making' anything. There's no goal to be reached; there's just the doing."

· · ·

The men took turns washing up in the kitchen. One evening as he did the dishes, Josh was looking out the window at Danny, who was standing in the yard, talking excitedly with his cell phone to his ear and a smile on his face. Josh felt a pang, knowing this was Danny's after-dinner time to gather lovingly with the wife and children he cherished. He felt no envy; he was glad for his friend's closeness with his family. But he grieved the loss of it for himself.

An idea came. *What am I doing, standing here feeling sorry?* He took out his phone and dialed a number. "Mom? It's Josh." There was a silence, then he heard May Lynk break down in tears. They had hardly talked since Grampa's death, and now he felt the glow of family love spreading through him. "Your sister's here," May said. "Let me put her on." Joshua's decision had brought him great comfort and pleasure.

. . .

An account of his deed at the lake had appeared in the local paper; now people were noticing and pointing to him when he went downtown. Some greeted him with smiles and stopped to chat. Hearing everyone call him Josh, he realized he'd adopted the name Joshua as a kind of protection when his troubles had come down. Now his boyhood name sounded new and different. At first he was wary of the attention, but then his isolation eased and he felt his heart open. *These are dear friends I once knew, and they're being so kind. Where have I been all my life? Into myself is the answer!*

One day he heard a knock at the door and went to open it. There stood old Gerwyn Jones, Grampa's best friend, with a big smile and a paper sack in his hand. Bent and white-bearded, his voice was somehow still very fresh and youthful-sounding. "Josh! So good to see you back! Can we have a visit?"

"Sure, sure. Please come in," Joshua said warmly, recalling the many musical treats with which this gifted flutist and Grampa had regaled him as a boy in this very house. He introduced Gerwyn to Danny and the three chatted for a while. Gerwyn said, "I've brought you something," He opened his sack and carefully drew out a very old phonograph record. "Your grampa and I recorded this old disc many years ago. I thought you might like to have it."

After Gerwyn left, Joshua recalled seeing an old portable phonograph under Grampa's bed when he was cleaning the cabin. He and Danny took the device out, wiped the dust off, and plugged it in. "It still works," Danny said. He peered at the handwritten label on one side of the record. *Ar Ben Waun Tredegar*, he read. "Wonder what that means."

"It means 'On Top of Tredegar Moor,'" said Joshua, remembering the rousing folk dance tune, once traditional in Wales. When it played and he heard Grampa chunking out the rhythm and chords for Gerwyn's rousing flute, he found his feet tapping in the old way.

The piece on the record's reverse side, labeled *Clychau Aberdyfi*, was unfamiliar to him. Grampa had included the title's translation as "The Bells of Aberdovey." As they listened to it, something in the tender melody stirred both men's imaginations.

"Grampa and Gerwyn had awesome chops!" Danny commented.

"They could play anything," Josh agreed, "and they were so humble about it."

"Okay, so what, if anything, do we do with this?"

"Hm. Maybe we don't do anything. Maybe we just enjoy it and perhaps learn something from it."

. . .

Josh's mother May came to visit for a few days. One evening as he was walking home from downtown, a chorus of voices sounded in his ears. Accompanied by a piano, people were singing one of his favorite songs, "Somewhere Over the Rainbow." He soon realized the music was coming from inside the cabin. Entering, he found his mother seated at Danny's keyboard. Around her stood a dozen or more people, most of whom he recognized. Their swelling voices filled the room, sounding like angels singing.

A heart-gladdening songfest followed, late into the night. Several people had brought instruments; one man strummed an old mandolin, and Gerwyn's flute was as lively as ever. A neighbor of Gerwyn's, a Mrs. Landrey, had accompanied her son to the event. Josh was aware of the thin teenage boy seated next to his mother; his attitude seemed jaded and lifeless. During an intermission the woman told Josh, "Harry's been teaching himself to play the guitar. He's wanting to ask you if you'll show him some things."

Josh held out his own guitar. "Why don't you first show me what you've learned?" he said.

Unsmiling, Harry Landrey took the instrument. It was evident to Josh that he knew how to hold it, but he was not prepared for what came next. Instead of fitting his fingers into the last frets in a beginner's C chord, Harry placed his left hand far up the fingerboard. Without any strain or difficulty, he began confidently picking Leonard Cohen's song "Hallelujah," backing the melody with occasional strumming of creative chords, blending the whole piece into a pleasing arrangement of his own. As Harry interpreted the song, Josh recognized that an unusual talent was before him. There was a hearty round of applause from everyone when the performance ended.

Josh said, "Did someone show you how to do that?" Harry shook his head no.

"And you want *me* to help *you*?"

The teen's bland face was suddenly lit with a smile. "Would you, sir?" he said.

Josh recognized that what was happening was another of those formative events whose significance he'd tended to miss along the way, but which as a student of Grampa's Way he had begun looking for. "Yes," he said. "But I think if I do, the learning will be happening on both sides." He then arranged for Harry to come the following day for what he called "a session, not a lesson."

. . .

That night Joshua lay awake in his bed, thinking of the old days. *Grampa, this did so much for me. It's like I'm stepping out into warm sunshine after a dream of sadness and loneliness. I know you're behind this, just as you've been behind all that's happened to me lately. Thank you, Grampa. I love you!*

"All this music!" Danny said at breakfast. "I mean, Grampa's poems, the record he made with Gerwyn, and the hoot last night. It's gotta add up to something."

"It does," Josh said.

"What, exactly?"

"I don't know. But I'm learning to go with what Lao Tzu says: 'A good traveler has no fixed plans, and is not intent on arriving.'"

As you live deeper in the heart,
the mirror gets clearer and clearer.

—*Rumi*

CHAPTER 11

REDEMPTION

J OSH HAD IMMERSED HIMSELF in what he called the "give-back," the unfettered joy that accrues for those who are gardeners of human possibility. Musical pieces and performances emerged now, not from his pen or guitar but from those of his students. Besides his musical activities, he found time to be a friend and mentor to a fatherless boy. He made regular visits to a sick old man whom May knew and who lived across the lake, reading to him and comforting him. He was holding the man's hand lovingly when he passed away.

His transformation of heart could not have helped but have an effect on those dearest to Josh. Beginning with an account of the water rescue, Danny's wife Marcia had kept Joy informed of the growth in her husband's spontaneous giving. One day when Christmas was approaching and a school vacation had begun, Josh heard a car pull up in the driveway. He looked out to see Joy, Beth, and Sarah Grace exiting Joy's van. He was overwhelmed. Not only was he unprepared for the visit; the stature of the girls reminded him of the breadth of time since he'd seen them.

"Hi, Josh!" Joy said. "Hi, Daddy!" shrieked the girls in unison. What was there to say? He hesitated, unsure of whether to close the distance. Then they rushed into his arms; Sweet Grace was first to reach him. Joy then came forward and, reaching over the children's heads, hugged her husband around the neck. Warm tears rushed up into his eyes.

Later they sat alone by the wood stove. "I once told you," Joy said, "to call me when you had something to say. I knew it was your bad feelings about yourself that kept you away. But 'actions speak louder,' as they say, and you've been communicating with me in the very best way you could. I couldn't be happier, dear, or more grateful."

Josh took every opportunity to get to know his girls. He recalled other conversations he'd had with Beth, whose forthrightness with him had always impressed him. Some of her words had been confrontations; he once remembered her innocent way of asking outright why he didn't want to be with the family. Now their talks were sharings; he was delighted with his daughter's intuitive grasp of the wisdom in Grampa's collection of quotations.

"You know, you're pretty smart," he told her one day.

"Sure. Like you," she said, smiling.

Josh also found himself admiring Sarah Grace's ways. Whereas Beth had always been regarded as "angelic," Sarah Grace was more playful and creative. Her brown eyes and light curls were often dancing with fun. The attitude was helpful for Beth's condition, but sometimes she would begin to wheeze. At the first sign that her sister was in trouble, Sweet Grace was immediately on the spot, holding her hand, bringing an atomizer or a cup of tea. "It's been like that ever since she was tiny," Joy told Josh. "She adores Beth. And her caregiving puts mine to shame."

A common sight in Tenby now was the pair, Josh and Sarah Grace, walking or skipping hand in hand through the snow and laughing. He would point to Ap Jack and say, "When spring comes, there's a place up there I want to take you to."

In his newfound fatherhood, Josh nourished a deep desire to instill the consciousness of Grampa in his youngest. She would say, "Tell me a Grampa story, Daddy," and he would draw from his vast collection. One day she said, "What did Grampa look like?" When Josh showed her the figure in the group photos, she said, "That's so small I can't see him." So he took out of his wallet a well-worn sketch that a friend had made and said, "That's what he looked like to me."

The girl gazed long at the picture. "He looks like a gentle rock," she said, then paused. "He looks like Ap Jack."

Harry Landrey began showing up on days other than his weekly "session" days. In time the reason was clear: he was smitten with Beth. He was now playing small gigs down in the city, and once Josh went with him and Beth to attend one. After the date, the three went to an all-night diner for dessert. Seated, Josh asked Harry, "How do you think it went?"

"Oh, not so well. I was nervous with you guys there, and I didn't think the band was good."

Beth reached out and took the boy's hand. "Harry," she said, "you were perfect. I am so proud of you. My dad told me you have a rare talent, but I got to see it for myself tonight." Her sincerity was unquestionable.

Tears stood in the young man's eyes. "Really?"

"Really!" Josh and Beth chorused.

"Never doubt it," Josh continued. "I've spent a lot of years second-guessing myself about whether I had what it takes, and I don't recommend spending a minute doing it." The boy nodded, and Josh went on: "I wouldn't say this to anyone who hadn't developed their craft, so they can trust it. Even though you're self-taught, I know you had to put in the time to get to where you are. So, here's a secret my grampa called journeying. It means if you just get out of the way and let your talent lead you, it takes you places. It's the opposite of what people do when they go through every day thinking *next, next,* always focusing ahead of where they are. Thinking only of next is deadly because you're trying to be someplace you're not. If you're patient, remain fully present in the moment, and refuse to rush, the music will come to you."

If you're patient, remain fully present in the moment, and refuse to rush, the music will come to you.

Harry's face lighted. "Wow, Mr. L.!" he said. "That is what it feels like. Thanks for naming it!"

. . .

The Christmas season held many reminders of the blessings that had come to Josh, Joy, Beth, and Sarah Grace. There was the trimming of the modest tree and the exchanging of small gifts, but all felt deeply that the greatest gift was their being together. One cold starry night they attended Tenby's annual Christmas tree lighting and sighed with the crowd when the lights went on. Walking home, Beth said, "This is the best Christmas we've ever had."

Sarah Grace said, "I know." Josh and Joy gazed at each other warmly.

One Saturday, Josh and Danny were alone in the cabin, the girls and their mother having gone to a party at Sarah Grace's friend's house. The men were tinkering with the guitar and keyboard when, unexpectedly, Gerwyn dropped by. Then May showed up.

Just then the phone rang. Josh showed amazement when he answered it. "I'll put you on speakerphone," he said, his face suddenly aglow. The voices that sounded were unrecognizable to those in the room. One had a decidedly Cockney accent. "Blimey, it's good to hear your voice, old mate!" Owen said. "Yeah," Toby said. "We've been thinking of you, and we really just wanted to say hi."

"All right," Josh said. "This is getting weirder and weirder. There are people here with me right now who have contributed so much to my life, in ways very similar to you two— as great musicians and even better friends. I want you to meet one another." He introduced each one, telling a little about the person in a warm and complimentary way.

Danny said, "I've got an idea Grampa is in this somehow."

"It's just like him," May agreed. "So, what do we do?"

After a silence, Josh reached under his chair and took out a cloth-wrapped object. He said, "I guess we're all here in some way to make music, and I thought I'd start by showing you something." He uncovered a beautiful mandolin. "Danny and I found this in the loft in Grampa's work shed." He explained what the item was to those on the phone. Then he took a pick from his pocket. "I've always thought of a mandolin playing bluegrass-style music," he said. "But I've been working a little on 'On Top of Tredegar Moor.' It starts like this." He played the first four bars.

Gerwyn said, "That's a good sound, Josh." Heads nodded, and Toby said, "Beautiful, dude! What are you thinking to do with it?"

"I don't know," Josh said. "I just like the tune, and the sound of the mandolin playing it."

Another quiet period ensued. Danny said, "Well, I could read something we found that Grampa wrote." He took a paper from the keyboard case and read Grampa's old "Made for Amazing" poem. The group sat again in silence until Josh said, "I think we're doing what Grampa would like—not acting like we know anything, but just being open and willing to be led. I say we just keep sharing and looking for clues."

Josh's words freed the process. One by one the others began to share their thinking. When evening came, they agreed they had done what they had come to do, without knowing beforehand. A new song had been born, titled, appropriately, "Emergence." They all marveled at the clarity with which the song came together on this frosty winter evening. Josh thanked each person as they left; his last words to the group were, "So glad you were here. Grampa definitely was."

. . .

The holidays were over. The girls were moody, regretting having to return home for school. As Joy finished packing she forced a smile. "Hard to leave." Walking to the door, she said, "I know you have unfinished work here, but it's going to be hard on us until you're home."

At the door, Josh embraced his family, feeling intensely the loss of a newly discovered world. "You all know I'll come as soon as I can," he said. He released them and they left the warmth of the cabin and ventured into the January chill.

At the car, Sarah Grace pleaded, "Please, Daddy, come with us."

Joy's eyes glowed across the space. He knew he would never get enough of the love he saw there.

"I miss you already, Dad," Beth said.

He watched the van drive away until it was out of sight—his girls' faces fading and Joy once again leaving him. An ache of separation settled over him, a sorrow unknown throughout his years on the road. Turning, he wandered back around the work shed, stopped, and looked up. Ap Jack's white peak clutched at the cold blue sky, seeming strangely a symbol of grief and aloneness.

Josh fell to his knees in the snow. A bottomless yearning clenched his heart for something he had never known the loss of. *I don't know who you are. I thought you were Grampa, but now I believe he was just working for you, speaking for you, teaching me to look for you. Grampa's just a part of you, as I am, as Joy and the kids are, as everything is.*

He bent over and down, somehow feeling the need to get as low as he could. *I want to see you, but you hide from me. I want to know you, but I don't know how.* He waited there until a trickle of peace came, a promise that the shade of grief would be appeased. *Anyway, we're talking now. Maybe that's the first step.*

People in Tenby knew of Josh's story as lead guitarist of a top band, and they thought of him as a sort of celebrity. Word spread that he was giving guitar lessons to Harry, and others wanted to learn from him as well. Soon Josh was giving weekly guitar lessons to Harry, three other boys, and one girl. This was welcome income, for his Christmas-time expenses with his family had diminished his funds. But it was not enough. Josh cast about for what to do to support himself.

One day he reluctantly wrapped the beautiful mandolin in its zippered cloth case and went to a pawn shop he had noticed at the other edge of town. He walked in, noting the suspicious glances he received from the old broker. Josh walked to the counter and took the instrument from its bag. He was keenly aware that an instrument of this quality was worth at least $5,000. Uttering an inner word of apology to Grampa, Josh cleared his throat.

"I'd like a loan of five hundred dollars on this," he said. "I'll want it back, of course."

The man scrutinized the instrument as if to find flaws with it. "Give you two hundred," he said.

Josh took the mandolin back and started to put it back in its cloth wrapper. "All right, two-fifty," the man said.

Josh shook his head in utter discouragement, but laid the precious bundle on the counter. "Like I said, I'll be back for it, soon."

"You've got one month," the man said.

"Why is that?"

"This is an expensive item," the man said crossly. "I can't be carrying it, waiting for you. If you don't come, and I get another offer for it, I will sell it."

"Trust me," Josh said firmly. "I will be back within a month." He took the receipt and left, feeling sorry to have left such a special new friend behind in such a tawdry-feeling place.

During the next weeks, a flu virus was working through the town. Josh had three students cancel their lessons for two straight weeks, all from sickness. He began to worry about his debt at the hockshop. At the month's end, he took himself back to the pawn shop to plead for more time. As he walked in, he saw that a young man had the mandolin out and was strumming it.

"Hey!" Josh shouted. "That's mine!"

"Not unless you have the money," the proprietor said. "This man wants it."

Josh lost control. "Well, he can't have it!" Advancing on the customer, he reached to grab the mandolin away. The man laid the instrument down on the counter to protect it, turned, and said calmly, "I have the cash to pay for it. Are you ready to reclaim it?"

"No!" Josh said. "I just need a few more days."

"Sorry," the broker said. "It goes to this man." He added in an unctuous tone, "Now, if you'll excuse us."

Josh flashed a look of hatred at the new owner of his grampa's prized mandolin. "I'm not through with you," he said loudly and stormed out of the shop. Walking home, his mind was full of vengeful thoughts.

. . .

As the hours went by, it seemed Josh could do nothing but mope and rage. The elation he had felt at his holiday reunion with his family was forgotten as his old self-blame leaked in around the edges of his consciousness. *Why is it always this way? Why can't I catch a break? I'm no good, that's why! I'll never be any good. Nothing ever seems to work out for me.* Despite the healing he had effected through his introspection and study, he felt helpless to stem the mental assault. It seemed his mind had descended into its old despair with one turn of the tide.

That night Josh hardly slept. He tossed and turned, his mind in a miasma of depression. In the morning, he rose and went to make coffee. Sitting at the kitchen table, his mind seemed to calm. He took a pad of paper and a pencil. It seemed he should write something. Or maybe draw something. He closed his eyes. *Grampa, it's you. Show me what to do. Please, Grampa, help me.* Slowly, in the screen behind his closed eyes, there emerged two rectangles. As he watched, he became aware of what they must be: a pair of choices. Opening his eyes, he drew two doors; one was so extremely wide as to appear unnatural, yet its glossy, veneered surface helped it to look comfortable and inviting. The other door was narrow, perched at the fringe of Josh's periphery, and had a simpler, more natural finish. On the left door, he placed a minus sign (–) and on the right a plus sign (+).

He sat looking at the picture of the left door and thought: *Very familiar. I know only too well what's behind that door: steps leading down to a cellar of depression and black moods. I've been there off and on for most of my life, and I've certainly been there this past day.*

Josh turned his attention to the door on the right. *Grampa, this is the door you want me to go through. It's about feeling good about myself. Not perfect, and certainly subject to mistakes and errors. I'm not 100 percent sure where this door leads, but something lies behind this door that means even if I fall flat on my face—and I will—it doesn't matter. Why? Because I* am a child of God. All I have to do is realize that fact, and troubles won't keep me down. Knowing I am a child of God makes me want to do better, to be my best, and to somehow make a positive difference in this world.

He smiled. Wow, Grampa. This is really not a very tough choice, right? I not only choose the plus door, I cross out the minus one! Even though I don't know the path ahead, I can never go wrong by picking the door on the right. The positive door is always the right door! With that Josh drew a large X over the left door.

The positive door is always the right door!

At that moment, the phone rang.

When he answered it, he recognized the caller's voice. "Is this Josh Lynk?"

"Yes."

"My name is Selwyn. Does that mean anything to you?"

"Sure. You're the guy who's got my mandolin."

"Well, yes. And I am actually calling about that. I wanted to tell you that when I got home with the mandolin yesterday my grandfather recognized it as one made by your grandfather, Bryn Lynk."

"Uh, that's right. But who—"

"I am Selwyn *Jones*. My grandfather is Gerwyn Jones."

Josh was stunned. "Wait. Of course! We used to know each other up here when we were boys!"

"That's right. How are you, Josh?"

Josh was performing a mental double take and at the same moment acknowledging the self-created upset with which he had been ruining the past twenty-four hours. "I'm fine, Sel. It's good to be talking to you." He paused. "And I certainly owe you an apology for the way I treated you in the store earlier."

"Ah, that's okay. I do want to talk with you about the mandolin because I'm sure it's a keepsake from your grandpa, and I want you to have it. We can work out the money."

"That's very good of you," Josh said humbly.

"And now, my grandpa, my wife Sally, and I want to invite you to dinner this evening. Can you come?"

Flabbergasted at the turn of events, Josh stammered his acceptance. The very enjoyable evening he spent with the Joneses turned out to be the rekindling of an old friendship.

The startling dream that had led to Josh's eventual return to Tenby kept coming to his mind. What had Grampa's words, "Head for Ap Jack," really meant? Was his daughter's comparison of the old man to the mountain a key? Maybe heading for Ap Jack meant going within, seeking solitude for the answer to himself. A quotation by Einstein kept coming to Josh: "We cannot solve our problems with the same thinking we used when we created them."

With the opening of Josh's sensibilities to embrace the world, new opportunities began to arise. Harry Landrey was the first of many talented young artists who came Josh's way to receive the gifts of his musical genius and his belief in them. He amassed a following as a soloist as well, and often gave small concerts to appreciative audiences. Dividing his energies between mentoring and performing, Josh soon became known as a top player-coach.

Spring announced its early arrival with a premature softening of Ap Jack Lake's icy top coat. Its melting now exposed a fluidity of movement that had always been lying just below the water's crusty surface. Spring also meant local community fundraising was in full bloom.

Knowing they had somewhat of a celebrity in their midst, the school board asked Josh to star in a benefit concert to help raise funds for building a new arts and sciences building at Beth's school. On the evening of the show, the place was packed.

Josh took the opportunity to play a wide variety of songs. He played a couple of old JLB tunes as well as an acoustic medley of Tawna hits. Josh also tested some newer pieces he had developed with May, Gerwyn, Danny, and local friends. He invited a few of his friends to join him on stage, and the audience responded favorably to fresh songs, "Peace, Be Still," "Give a Little," "Alive Again," "Always Within Me," and "Just Believe."

Halfway through the program, his listeners were absorbed in Josh's solo version of "Emergence." Just as the song was concluding, the crowd saw Josh stop unexpectedly. He was standing there silently, as if deep in thought. He seemed to be listening.

I see now, Grampa, what you meant. It's suddenly so clear to me; how could I not have seen it before? The song you always told me to find was not music at all. It was the essence of what I am. My very being was the song all along, right? Right.

That was when the melody found him.

My very being was the song.

Placing the guitar he had been using in a stand, Josh went to the rear of the stage and took another instrument from a battered case. The way he handled it, it was evident that this was an old friend—his Old Warrior. After making slight tuning adjustments, he closed his eyes and seemed to be waiting. The silence was audible.

Slowly the notes emerged of a song no one, including himself, had ever heard before. Josh was blessed, for behind his closed eyes he felt certain people tuning in. He knew Joy, the girls, and Harry were out in the crowd watching. But Mr. C., Danny, Gerwyn, and his mother were also present, their faces lit with smiles as they witnessed the revelation unfolding. Even Toby and Owen had flown in secretly to see Josh and to offer their support for the school's fundraiser. One other individual, of course, was there, his loving spirit hallowing all the rest: Grampa.

Audience members would later talk about that evening with great wonder, and friends would often ask them to tell about the experience. For the song that found Josh Lynk on that stage would soon become the iconic song of the year, one of the most memorable titles of the decade. Everywhere people went, they heard it. They sang it, they hummed it and repeated its words, taking their meaning in hungrily. Its popularity attested to a time when the human spirit was broken and needed nourishing.

. . .

For Josh, something that occurred after the concert would affect him for a long time. Immediately after the song ended, the school principal, Mrs. Jaffe, came onstage, thanked Josh warmly, and led a huge round of applause. As the cheering died and he came down off the stage, a crowd of people moved forward to group around him. The song had done something to them, and they didn't know how to respond to it except by moving toward the source. The faces Josh was looking at were reflections of the radiant mood the closing song had created. A curious hush prevailed. The glowing eyes of the fans evidenced the heart-opening impact of the music.

"Where can I get a copy of that?" was the question on most lips. Josh was at a loss. "I'll, I'll just have to . . . write it down," he stammered. "That's the best I can tell you." People smiled and looked at one another. One said, "See? I told you he was composing it, right up there on stage!"

As people began to move away, still in a kind of thoughtful glow, Josh looked up to see loving gazes from his family—both from his own mother and from Joy. But he was shocked to also see his friends from the Tawna days, Toby and Owen. They grabbed him and hugged him hard, then stood back stammering with tears in their eyes, as if they couldn't find the words.

"I can't tell you, man," Toby said." "That song . . ."

"No words, mate," Owen mumbled.

Then came the most unexpected event of all. Saying, "We have a surprise for you!" Owen pulled someone out of the crowd who had been hanging back.

"Bill!" Josh yelled.

Indeed, Bill Joist was there, smiling in an unusual way. In fact, his entire presentation was changed. Gone were the bags under his eyes. His skin glowed; his posture was alert. "You look . . . different!" Josh said, to the laughter of his old bandmates. "Don't 'e look a bit cleaner to yer?" Owen put in. Bill's embarrassed grin allowed Josh to respond. "You do, Bill. You look so good!" he said, and the two hugged.

"Been months since I've had a drink," Bill said a bit sheepishly, "or anything, for that matter. I've started working out, eating better. Hey, I'm even meditating!" Now feeling the need to make a joke in the old way, Bill added, "After all, this world of clean and sober has me totally confused. I just can't keep up with it!" The group broke out in laughter at the lighthearted comment. The warmth surrounding the men was palpable.

Josh was curious about his friend's transformation. "What caused all this, Bill?"

Bill's tone was calm and straightforward. "You did, my friend."

"Me?"

"You were my inspiration. I just watched you through those days, being yourself without apology, standing for the light through all the wildness and craziness of the band. You never preached at us nor blamed us, but instead you were all about simple goodness. My life is better because you were in it. So I just came here to thank you."

Joy and the girls had heard this exchange. Now they moved up and hugged the Tawna players. To Joy's offer for them to stay overnight, they shook their heads. "That's very kind," Toby said, "but we have to catch a plane." With a glance at Josh, he added, "You know Tiny!"

. . .

Josh had plenty to think about. Lying awake that night, listening contentedly to Joy's breathing, he talked to Grampa. *I know you're pleased, Grampa. The change in Bill alone is enough to have made the entire evening. But doing the song on stage was such a gift. I saw what it did to the people, and I know the words and music came straight from you. So, like I told Toby that time, I'll have your name on the music.*

But where does something like that come from, really? Nobody owns it. It just comes through someone—happened to be me tonight. And you were there to help me journey and get out of its way.

None of us can say when our deepest truth will find us. For Josh, it occurred when he was in his element, performing music. It was not on a big concert stage in Seattle that it came, or even in the local music theater of his hometown. The auditorium of his daughter's middle school was where that truth descended on Josh, and it had a powerful and lasting outcome.

Why had this man, this unbelievably gifted musician, gone through his life not believing in himself? Perhaps it was to reach so many others around the world who don't believe, who so easily doubt, and who rarely try to bring from their own depths something unique and positive for the world. Why, Josh is singing to *us*! His song is for *us*.

In the years that followed, Joshua Lynk came to appreciate every moment of the doubts and fears he had put himself through, for they enabled him to discover a song that would eventually comfort and heal so many other souls.

Countless times Josh would find himself looking back at his journey in wonder and amazement. And, each time, two humble words would rise spontaneously from his heart: "Thank you."

Thank You.

The only person you are destined to become is the person you decide to be.

—*Ralph Waldo Emerson*

EPILOGUE

A FEW MONTHS AFTER Josh's performance at his daughter's school, he began to reflect on how his journey had shaped him, and what the future might hold for him. The open question circulating through his mind was sharpened when Harry Landrey approached him one fall afternoon.

"So, how do you think it all fits together?" Harry asked innocently.

"Sorry, what do you mean?" came Josh's reply.

Harry responded with slightly more detail. "I mean, how do you think your story helped to bring you where you are today, and what will you do with it from here?"

Seeming curious, but still not sure how to respond, Josh leaned in. "I don't know, Harry. I guess a lot of it came through the support of Grampa, my mother, and Joy, among others. Plus, loads of sacrifice, practice, and a simple desire to be part of something more, something bigger than myself.

I guess I was looking for some deeper purpose to my life and my leadership."

Harry reflected silently for a moment. "So, it sounds like the key to it all was in your desire for a purpose, and to find deeper meaning which guided your leadership, right? If that's the case, then what is that deeper meaning you found—I mean, what is your leadership purpose?"

"Hm. I dunno," Josh chuckled as he shrugged. The question seemed simple enough, but the answer? Not so much. "I think for me it's about helping people, and playing music, writing positive stuff."

"So, your leadership purpose is helping people, then? Through music, and being positive?"

"Yeah, that's it. Say, how's *your* practice going these days? Working on any new tunes?" Josh hoped his admittedly canned response would satisfy Harry, and his own question back to Harry would successfully deflect and reposition the conversation.

"Oh, it's going OK." Harry smiled and nodded. "However, what's most important to me is not writing great songs. I want to find some purpose to my leadership that drives *everything*, something that *writes me*. A leadership purpose that grips me from deep within and shapes my destiny. I want to feel it make sense and come together, like my own tailored suit. If I find *that* . . . then I'm convinced the great songs will write themselves."

Josh later reflected on his conversation with Harry, admitting to himself that he felt a bit stumped by Harry's questions regarding leadership purpose. Josh could certainly recall his own life story, his strengths and weaknesses, and he knew how he felt about his leadership purpose. However, he hadn't really captured anything like the concept Harry described, the idea he had sought so passionately.

When Harry added "destiny" into the mix, it complicated the topic even further; however, thinking of the word led Josh to recite aloud a simple phrase: "Destiny is not so much what happens *to* us; destiny is what happens *because* of us."

Destiny is not so much what happens *to* us; destiny is what happens *because* of us.

Had Grampa said that before? Or did I just make it up? Regardless, the pronouncement sparked action.

Josh decided to take the time to chronicle his own journey more carefully, looking for clues that would help him to assemble a more powerful authentic leadership purpose statement. He began putting the pieces of his life together, and things started to make more sense. He cycled through a few piecemeal efforts to capture and refine his purpose statement—the personal identifier, upon which his entire existence was built—and he eventually tapped into something which grabbed him in a unique and powerful way.

Josh's final statement read:

> ## MY AUTHENTIC LEADERSHIP PURPOSE
>
> *To be the maestro of the heart, calling you on a journey to open the right door, come outside, break through the ice, and discover the wellspring in your soul. To help you scale the peaks, find your joy, be filled with grace, find strength for the climb, and believe.*

Josh paused to reread the written credo resting comfortably in front of him. Reflecting on his sharpened sense of leadership purpose, Josh knew now—without question—he was *home*.

I cannot teach anybody anything.
I can only make them think.

—*Socrates*

QUESTIONS FOR REFLECTION
AND DISCUSSION

The questions below may help you to reflect on and discuss each chapter. Some questions relate directly to the storyline itself, while others are more self-reflective in nature. These questions are not meant to represent an exhaustive list; rather, the intent is to bring a few key topics to light in a way that will ignite your thinking and accelerate your own journey toward greater authentic leadership purpose.

A couple of points are worth noting here. First, you should not feel obligated to answer every question, as these are simply representative samples to spark your imagination and guide your critical thinking. Second, you may find questions you are not yet prepared to answer nor address fully at a given time. This is very natural, as many questions deal with much weightier topics than you might have noticed in the storyline. Please do not let any open questions keep you from reading the story in its entirety! Understanding Josh's complete journey is critically important, just as it is important to understand your own work and life in its entirety.

After reading the book and addressing the related questions, my hope is that you will arrive with a much greater sense of what makes you *amazing* as well as a clearer sense of what makes those key people around you amazing. In addition, my intent is to help you discover, sharpen, and amplify your authentic leadership purpose. If you would like additional details or a more extensive guide to support your efforts, then please feel free to explore the companion workbook and materials which supplement the book.

I wish you all the very best on your journey!

CHAPTER 1

1. What music brings out the deepest emotions in you?

2. Who was (or is) your "Grampa"? What (or where) is your "Ap Jack Mountain"?

3. How do think Josh feels when we first meet him? What tones do you see and hear resonating from his spirit?

4. What "gifts" did you inherit in your youth?

5. What dreams haunt you? Are they dreams of something that occurred, or something you wanted to happen (but remains unfulfilled)?

6. Are you *in tune*? How does your life's music sound?

CHAPTER 2

1. When do you feel a song flowing freely through your life and work?

2. What natural talents, skills, and abilities are you developing actively and practicing intentionally? What is your motivation for each key talent and skill you're working to develop?

3. Why did Mr. C. tell Josh there was a seat inside him, but it was an empty chair?

4. Who is your "Danny," someone representing a strong and stable friend in your life? Who is your Maestro? Are there a few?

5. How beautiful and powerful is the music you orchestrate with your teammates, both inside and outside of work?

6. What do you tell yourself when no one else is listening?

CHAPTER 3

1. How have your life experiences "shaped" you? Your top three or four successes? Your top three or four challenges?

2. In what parts of your work and life would you like to "true up"? Do you have a vision for what you would like the result of your work and life to be?

3. When do you feel you are in the flow? When you're "being played"? How does it feel when you're there?

4. Are you playing others' music, or your own? What "show tunes and cover songs" are you performing?

5. Are there any "diseases" (read: dis-ease) that threaten your personal life and leadership purpose? Have you ever reached the point where you feel you are "suffocating, or drowning"? How do you react or cope?

6. Your life is a "one-take recording"; if you could "record anything," then what would it be?

CHAPTER 4

1. What did you play with all your heart and soul as a child? In your teen or young adult years?

2. Have you ever felt a door open to something amazing inside you? What was it? How did it make you feel?

3. Has "something larger" been calling out to you? Is it a higher calling or a siren song? What's the difference?

4. What "optics" have tried to lure you in with hopes of fame, fortune, success, recognition, or happiness? Have you ever experienced an "optical illusion"?

5. Have you ever been in a situation where your values were questioned, were tested, or caused serious loss? What happened? How did it impact you?

6. Would you have taken Tiny G's deal? Why or why not? How would you have *evaluated* (i.e., tested against your *values*) your decision?

CHAPTER 5

1. What has caused fear in your work life before, and why did you feel fearful? Was it validated? How did the experience that followed work out?

2. What makes you want to "sing the blues"? How prevalent are they in your work repertoire? At home?

3. Does it seem logical that Josh would be most drawn to Toby? Why or why not?

4. What "song in your heart" makes you feel so touched that you revel in it—it's strong enough to make you laugh or cry with its emotional power?

5. When were your values at odds with those across your team or company? Can you describe a situation where your needs and values came under attack?

6. Where and when do you feel intimacy with *yourself*? Do you think it is important?

1. How does Josh's time with Grampa compare to his younger years? After the fight in the tavern, why did Josh choose not to call Grampa? What would you have done?

2. What did Joy mean when she recalled Grampa's statement, "Your environment is often stronger than your willpower"? Have you ever mapped the connection between your actions, relationships, and the presence of joy in your own work and life?

3. What types of "influences" are you under? Are they healthy? Are there disruptions that surround you, threatening to keep your life in conflict?

4. Are you working on unique "arrangements," or lured by "corporate" emphasis on following the latest sizzle? Is there any relationship between busyness, pressure, focus on what's popular, and your work?

5. In what "journeys" do you become lost in the moment, yielding wholeheartedly to inspiration? Where you feel like something special is coursing through you, and you're "just listening and following along?"

6. Do you see any relationship between "Born Knowing" and "Generosity"? Do you think there is any linkage? What was Josh Lynk's role in helping these two new (and very different) Tawna songs come about? What were you "born knowing"?

CHAPTER 7

1. Does Toby have any choice but to tolerate the Tawna band members? What are you tolerating in your own life, and what are your tolerance levels?

2. Have you "lost touch" with anyone critically important to your life? Are there any areas of your work or life where your silence has led to a place where you feel isolated, confined, or "imprisoned"?

3. How often do you practice "deep listening"? When have answers simply "come to you," just in time?

4. Whenever possible, Grampa always imparted spiritual concepts and wisdom to Josh. Was the final interaction between Grampa and Josh devoid of spiritual insight?

5. If you left this earth today, what special "songs" would still be left inside you, unplayed? What music does your spirit yearn to perform before the curtain is drawn? What will you be remembered for when you are gone?

6. What is your *Leadership Purpose* at this moment in your life? What principles would you tell Grampa are guiding your life? Write it down, even if it's a work in progress.

CHAPTER 8

1. How often do you return home, where you grew up, or to your family and old friends? Do you sometimes feel like a "visitor" in your own skin, away from your own "home" too frequently? How do you get back?

2. When has despair strengthened you to take action and create something new? Name one work and personal situation. How did the difficulty lead to an eventual turnaround or new opportunity?

3. When faced with the apparent choice between Tawna and Joy, Joshua chose Joy. How often do you face a challenge and choose to sacrifice joy? Do you believe joy is something you can keep close to you daily?

4. Do you ever feel a "knocking" on your wall, in your head, or in your heart? What, or who, is it, and how loudly do you hear it? If this "knocking" had a voice, what would it be telling you right now?

5. To what, or whom, are *you* a "link"; i.e., the one who represents strength during trials, and hope for freedom and a better life?

6. What separations in your work, life, and/or relationships can you begin to narrow or close?

1. Why did Josh feel the need to return to Ap Jack? Why was it a solo journey, and how did he spend his time once there? How often do you retreat, completely alone, to be still and practice deep listening?

2. What role does nature play, if any, in finding places to be still and reflect? What are your favorite natural elements—those that soothe your soul the most? The mountains, a river or lake, the beach, a forest, etc.?

3. How did Grampa "reveal" himself to Josh, upon Josh's return to Ap Jack? What "signs" surround your life, pointing you to something deeper, richer, and better? Have you stopped to read them, and can you hear what they have been telling you? What signs are making themselves known to you now?

4. How important are spiritual matters in your life? Do you notice any connection or relationship between spiritual wellness and overall health in your work and/or personal life?

5. What role did The Tree play in the lives of Grampa and Josh? How does it protect, nourish, and grow

you? What new root systems must you develop and grow to prepare you for your future journeys?

6. Name three or four people you think are amazing. What makes them amazing in your eyes? How do you help others to see and feel "they are (made for) amazing, too"?

What do you think makes *you* amazing?
List at least three or four things below. Be generous!!

CHAPTER 10

1. How often is Josh playing during this "stage" of his life? What is he writing—is it changing at all?

2. Do you keep a journal? Where do you capture your thoughts, ideas, and things that inspire you? What patterns do you see emerging?

3. "Journeying" is a way of following a melody's inner path; therefore, joy and grace are likely found in the journeying itself. How is your journey going so far? Do you sense joy and grace frequently and strongly?

4. How "full of yourself" are you? How often do you practice the art of "emptying yourself" (e.g., selfish desires, improper motives, ego-driven wants, unresolved guilt, lack of forgiveness, etc.)?

5. Josh fulfills an ancient exhortation to "be strong and courageous." Is it surprising that he does this by saving another's life, versus blazing a trail in his own?

6. How and when do you practice "selfish unselfishness"? What do you do for others, both at work and in your personal life? When, and why, do you enjoy giving to and/or helping others?

CHAPTER 11

1. With Tawna, Josh feared he was conforming to their likeness. Now, we see Josh undergoing a transformation of heart. What made the difference; what changes in Josh do you see?

2. The first part of journeying means to "get out of the way." What does this mean to you? How useful is it to "just be open and remain willing to be led?" Do you believe if you're fully present, yielded and still, patient, and refusing to rush, the music comes to you?

3. Josh unexpectedly chooses a mandolin to play with his family and friends, leading to the development of a ground-breaking new song. What new things have you tried, to shake up your own routines, or to gain new perspective?

4. What dreams and natural talents have you "pawned," placing them on hold in exchange for a quick (but paltry) payout? Which of these prized possessions do you feel at risk of losing (perhaps for good)? Have unexpected events caused you to delay reclamation of your own priceless assets?

5. After Josh's wife and kids left, what led him to fall to the ground and engage some deeper source in a conversation? What was he asking; what was he seeking?

6. Josh says, "The *right* door is always the *positive* door." Do you agree with this statement? Why or why not?

EPILOGUE—PUTTING THE PIECES TOGETHER

1. Clues are not overtly recognized—by definition, they must be discovered. How do you incorporate sharing and looking for clues in your own life? Have you identified clues to your leadership and life purpose?

2. Josh's last-referenced original song appeared to have been birthed in real-time. How many elements and circumstances were present that led to the revelation of this iconic song?

3. Do you believe in a sense of destiny? Do you feel Josh was fulfilling his destiny at some point in the story? If so, then how much of his destiny "came to him," as a pre-determined course, and how much emerged via his actions and efforts?

4. What destiny will happen *because of you*?

5. What is *your* voice? What is *your song*? What will *you sing* boldly to the world?

Based on what you have read, and your responses to the discussion questions, attempt to refine and describe your Leadership Purpose below.

MY LEADERSHIP PURPOSE

_____

_____

_____

_____

_____

_____

_____

_____

To see other examples of Leadership Purpose, and to share your own, please visit: www.madeforamazing.com/ leadershippurpose

ACKNOWLEDGMENTS

My acknowledgments would be the size of a book, if I had space! Special thanks to those who were instrumental in shaping this book:

To Steve and Marilyn Nation, for being amazing in your own special ways, for everything you've done for me, and for always being there.

To Leslie, for your patience and adventurous spirit. You are more amazing than you will ever know—believe it!

To Madeline and Alex, the most incredible kids a father could hope for. Your talents and hearts inspire me daily, and I'm excited to see what God will do with and through each of your lives. I'm so proud of you!

To Alison and Allen Pilkington, for your spiritual discernment and strength which so often kept me going. To Ashley, Joey, Laura, Christian, Darrell, and Karen Demastus, for overall awesomeness!

To Chris Nation, for more than I can say (or anyone would understand!). Love you, bro.

To James and Sana Sutton, for your prayers, support, and steadfast faith. To Jamie and Kelly Smith, for your friendship and encouragement over the years.

To Mary Brabston, Howard Finch, Marilyn Helms, Frank Williamson, and Monique Berke, for your advocacy in the early days, guiding me toward a trajectory that changed the course of my life. To Jay and Mark Lewis, for our great talks and your positive spirits.

To Nick Craig and Authentic Leadership Institute, Steve Byrum and Bill Wilson, and HBS professors Michael Porter, Joe Badaracco, Clay Christensen, Rosabeth Moss Kanter, Tom DeLong, Scott Snook, and Bill George, for your thought leadership.

To Tanya, Justin, Carrie, Jen, Brian, Steven, Kristine, and the Greenleaf Book Group, for a great experience.

To Rick Nash, for your collaboration and selfless commitment; I'm incredibly grateful. To Johnnie Moore and the Kairos Company, for your leadership.

To innumerable HBS friends, especially Shauna, Dan, Bratko, Andrew, Jason, Bernshteyn, Foley, Julia, Adam, Jess, Matt, Derek, Caroline, Leonora, Chris, Ryan, Krebs, Defriese, Anne, Tina, Tonio, Amit, Charles, Samantha, AnaMaria, and many others who supported the journey.

To colleagues, global leaders, or friends who were a sounding board: Bron, Elbert, John, Shailesh, Rohit, Juan, James, Diego, Judd, Jason, Xiao Hui, Jenny, Caroline, David, Judith, Sophia, Max, Ocean Li, Eugene, Louis, George, Sheri, Luka, Evie, and Chase, Weidner, Guilloux, Hill, Asher, Mitchell, Ackerman, Chang, and Head families.

To Jim Ballard and Barbara Perman, for your friendship, coaching, and encouragement.

To Frank and Charlie Brock, Richard Floyd, Tom Francescon, Mike Bradshaw, Jack, Allison, Ashlee and CO.LAB, Mickey at Vayner, Bob and Clark at J103, Sandra, Jim and Brewer Media, Mark Love from Sprocket/Journey Church, Andy Perez, David Belitz, Cordell Carter, Will Joseph, Rick and Willa at Chambliss, Jonathan and Sheldon, Miller Welborn, Philip Hare, and CBMC, Tennessee Christian and Chattanooga Chambers.

To authors, pastors, and musicians Andy Stanley, John Ortberg, Crawford Lorritts, Rob Morgan, Mark Batterson, Banning Liebscher, Brad and Esme Warne, SQuire Rushnell, Parker Palmer, Randy Street, Chip Bell, Barry Banther, Third Day, MercyMe, Journey, Lincoln Brewster, Hillsong, Natalie Grant, Colton Dixon, Jordan Feliz, Chris Tomlin, Christian Stanfill, Bethel Music, Michael W. Smith, and Steven Curtis Chapman.

To Michael Kendrick, David Carr, Warren Radtke, Jonathan Merkh, Joel Kneedler, Peter Lowe, Brad Lomenick, Michael Drew, Charlie Fusco, Roy H. Williams, Brian Mitchell, Kathy Helmers, Cinde Dobson, Becky Robinson, David Ratner, Jayme Johnson, Cole, Kristen, Liz and Alison, Carolyn, David, Brian and Sharon, for offering wise counsel.

To Almighty God: The best gift has been to know You more, and for this I save the greatest thanks for last. Thank You for collaborating with me so closely and the incredible times we share together. The Ultimate Positive Door!

ADDITIONAL RESOURCES FOR
MADE FOR AMAZING

Free Coaching—If you are a business owner or executive, I would like to offer you a free 30-minute executive coaching session as my way of saying thanks. Share your biggest personal or professional challenge with me at **VIP@NationLeadership.com**, and we will address it during our phone or video consultation together.

Free Assessments—Take the *Sound Check* to determine your readiness for larger stages. Access other surveys and assessments to tune up and amplify your life.

Get Inspired—Share Your Story. Inspire Others. Learn from others' leadership transformation stories. Tell us about your own journey and the challenges you have overcome (or are working through) to discover and embrace your authentic leadership purpose.

Individual and Group Study Materials—Learn more about Mark's ideas for the book, key characters, and important themes that will inform your transformation journey. View videos and Q&A guides to facilitate Book Clubs and Individual or Group Study.

Resources—Find book-related materials, gifts, apparel, and accessories to make your business, team, and community even more amazing.

Join the Conversation—Connect with Mark and others at MadeForAmazing.com as well on Facebook, Twitter, and YouTube to receive updates, special offers, and ongoing inspiration. Share book samples, book tweets, and graphics cards.

Tell Someone, "You Are Amazing!" Today—Take the opportunity to encourage someone every day. Post short messages here, and access pre-formatted email templates for quick and effective re-use throughout the year.

www.MadeForAmazing.com

THE *MADE FOR AMAZING* PARTICIPANT'S GUIDE

In this powerful booklet, Mark Nation helps you unlock your heart's deepest desires and unleash your authentic leadership purpose for maximum impact. The *Made for Amazing* Participant's Guide is packed with additional questions and exercises to support personal reflection, and plenty of space to allow freedom of thought and movement. Mark utilizes insights from Joshua Lynk's journey and decades of global experience to serve as your personal executive guide—allowing you to develop, refine, and sharpen your leadership purpose. Mark helps you shape your purpose into specific, concrete action plans that become your written record for dreaming big and preparing for a life of significance and satisfaction.

The *Made for Amazing* Participant's Guide is designed to supplement *Made for Amazing* and can be used for individual or group discussions and team workshops.

THE *MADE FOR AMAZING* VIDEO CURRICULUM

This dynamic video curriculum helps participants understand how to develop authentic leadership purpose, find their "song" in work and life, and create a long-term plan to share these unique gifts boldly with the world. Mark Nation serves as your personal executive coach, guiding you on the journey to build an amazing career and a life of deep significance. Each section wraps up with practical advice on how to put your leadership purpose into action. Available as a pack that includes one softcover Participant's Guide and one DVD.

Video sessions include:

- Chapter Summaries and Teachable Moments
- Key Concepts for Authentic Leadership Purpose
- Introductions to Participant's Guide Exercises
- Instructions for Course Leaders
- Bonus Material: Q&A with Mark, Behind-the-Scenes Footage

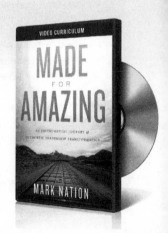

Also Available: Curriculum Kit, which includes one hardcover book, one DVD containing video sessions, a getting started guide for leaders and participants, and collectible bracelets to share with your team. The curriculum can be used to manage team workshops, small group studies, and for individual use.

THE *MADE FOR AMAZING* PROJECT

The *Made for Amazing* Project mission is to inspire others to live with authenticity and a greater sense of purpose. We encourage those who feel they have no special voice to believe. To reclaim a spirit of imagination. To dream, develop, grow, and innovate. We want to reach 10 million people worldwide with a very personal message:

Your **Life Matters.**
You are **Designed for a *Purpose*.**
You are **MADE for *AMAZING*.**

As part of our objective, we seek to develop 100,000 authentic leaders who dedicate their unique gifts to improve the quality of life for others around the world. Upon completing this book, *you should now be one of these leaders.*

JOIN IN OUR EFFORT

The *Made for Amazing* Project is looking for individuals, families, businesses, foundations, churches, and synagogues who care deeply about people to join our Support Team. To fulfill our mission, we need your assistance. Here are a few ways you can help:

- Commit to investing in and developing at least 10 people, utilizing the tools and techniques found in this book and supplemental resources.
- Invite Mark to speak at your school, church, synagogue, or association.
- Make a donation to support free books and workshops to those in need, who feel they have no voice (e.g., high-risk schools, emerging countries, those facing serious physical or emotional health challenges, etc.).
- Offer an in-kind contribution to support selling, general, and administrative functions (e.g., marketing, social media, advertising, etc.).
- Serve as an *Amazing Ambassador*, on a local, national, or international basis.

Through our fiscal sponsors, donations are tax-exempt and qualify as charitable deductions for US federal income tax purposes.

**Our dream is to help 10 million people find their song and
sing it boldly with the world.**

www.MadeForAmazingProject.com

KEYNOTES, SEMINARS, AND WORLD-CLASS AUTHENTIC LEADER DEVELOPMENT

MADE FOR AMAZING—Finding Your Song in Work and Life. Each of us has a song to sing to the world—it's the essence of whom we really are. In this powerful presentation, Mark shares how music metaphors can be used to deepen our authentic leadership purpose, and tune our careers for success. Ancillary executive coaching and team workshops are available; sessions vary from 2.5 hours to 1.5 days.

ADDING VALUE—A Nobel Prize Decision-Making Approach. We all know strong values are important, but can values really be used to make better decisions in the workplace? Isn't it enough to have a high IQ, emotional balance, and a good personality? In this engaging presentation, Mark uncovers how sustained good judgment is the key to individual and organizational success. He shares how the work of a Nobel Prize-nominated philosopher is being used to turbocharge leadership decisions. A variety of values-driven assessments are available to supplement the keynote, or via separate coaching and team workshops.

ALIGNED FOR LIFE—The Incredible Power of Unity in Business. It's not enough to define business strategy and assume it will work; only 14 percent of employees understand their firm's strategy. In this insightful talk, Mark reveals the Keys to Strategy Execution (KSEs), and shares how ground-breaking Harvard Business School work led to software that drives superior alignment and results. Alignment assessments are available to supplement the keynote or via coaching and team workshops.

ADDITIONAL SPEAKING TOPICS

- Building a Legacy That Lasts
- Leading Business and Career Change
- Building Winning Teams and Relationships
- Turbocharge Your Hiring: Boardroom to Mailroom
- Amplify Results Through Partners
- Keeping the Faith @ Work

- Purpose-Driven Sales and Service
- *Amazing* Business Development
- *Amazing* Personal and Corporate Branding
- Leading Across Countries and Cultures
- The Power of Pause
- Spiritual Values in Business

For more information, or to schedule Mark to speak to your organization, contact **info@NationLeadership.com**, or visit **www.MarkNation.net**.

NATIONLEADERSHIP ❯❯

Nation Leadership is built around one, simple concept: *It is ALL about people*. We are 100% focused on the power center at the heart of business, and that is *always* a matter of people development. We work with individuals, teams, executives, and partners to inspire business with more vision, purpose, passion, engagement, and positive drive. We develop high-integrity leaders who maintain strong values aligned to their firm's core mission, and strive to make excellent decisions that benefit all stakeholders.

Simply put: We help you to outperform your competition. We bring your strategy to life, in close collaboration with you, and in partnership with your most prized asset: *your people*.

❯❯ **ASSESSMENTS** Measure scores for yourself, your team, and key relationships across leadership, decision-making, innovation, engagement, sales and service capacity, safety, and athleticism. Identify and foster strengths, while improving weaknesses.

❯❯ **CONSULTING** Partner with global experts to unleash the creative potential and energy inside you, your team, and your company. We measure and optimize your positive impacts, from boardroom-to-mailroom, and to your clients.

❯❯ **COACHING** Connect with business leaders and coaches who understand your challenges and support your transformation. Specialties include authentic leader development, value-based decision-making, international management, personal branding, and change management.

❯❯ **TRAINING** Sharpen your skills and learn best practices across virtually every aspect of the people-centric value chain. We are wholly-focused on helping you to become an authentic, purpose-driven leader.

❯❯ **RESOURCES** Access leadership materials, study guides, coaching tips, videos, newsletters, and more. Read Mark's blog for his latest thoughts on leadership.

❯❯ **EVENTS** Gain valuable hands-on experience at one of our live events, seminars, and workshops.

NATION LEADERSHIP
P.O. Box 24476, Chattanooga, TN 37422
www.NationLeadership.com | 423.847.2678

ABOUT THE AUTHOR

 Mark Nation is a globally recognized management expert, leadership consultant, executive coach, author, and speaker. He is personally driven to discover what makes individuals, teams, and organizations *amazing*—those elements that power the heart and soul of individuals and businesses worldwide.

Mark is Founder and President of Nation Leadership, the Made for Amazing Project, and Harvard Help Circle. He has developed and managed companies in five industries: enterprise technology, financial services, music and entertainment, construction, and professional services. He has led start-ups and served in key regional or global executive roles at SAP, JDA Software, Siebel Systems (Oracle), and UNUM. Mark has developed people, products, and partnerships on six continents, gaining experience in virtually every function across the business value chain. His work has been leveraged across a wide range of clients, from young leaders, corporate managers, and executives, to Fortune 500 organizations, start-ups, schools, churches, and non-profits.

Mark graduated *summa cum laude* from the University of Tennessee at Chattanooga, and holds an MBA from Harvard Business School. He is a former professional musician and Ironman triathlete, still enjoying skiing, running, and biking when possible. His work and travels have taken him to more than forty US states and thirty-five countries, where he has managed, performed, or spoken to over 300,000 people. When not traveling, Mark is based in Tennessee.

Mark would love to connect with you. You can reach him directly at:

Email: mark@nationleadership.com
Twitter: @MarkNation
LinkedIn: Mark Nation
Facebook: Mark Nation